Genetic Dilemmas

D0834269

Genetic Dilemmas

Reproductive Technology, Parental Choices, and Children's Futures

Second Edition

DENA S. DAVIS

OXFORD
UNIVERSITY PRESS
2010

OXFORD
UNIVERSITY PRESS

Oxford University Press, Inc., publishes works that further
Oxford University's objective of excellence
in research, scholarship, and education.

Oxford New York
Auckland Cape Town Dar es Salaam Hong Kong Karachi
Kuala Lumpur Madrid Melbourne Mexico City Nairobi
New Delhi Shanghai Taipei Toronto

With offices in
Argentina Austria Brazil Chile Czech Republic France Greece
Guatemala Hungary Italy Japan Poland Portugal Singapore
South Korea Switzerland Thailand Turkey Ukraine Vietnam

Published by Oxford University Press, Inc.
198 Madison Avenue, New York, New York 10016
www.oup.com

Oxford is a registered trademark of Oxford University Press.

Library of Congress Cataloging-in-Publication Data
Davis, Dena S., 1947-
Genetic dilemmas : reproductive technology, parental choices, and
children's futures / Dena S. Davis. — 2nd ed.
p. ; cm.
Includes bibliographical references and index.
ISBN 978-0-19-537438-4
I. Title.
[DNLM: 1. Genetic Counseling.   2. Genetic Diseases,
Inborn—prevention & control.   3. Genetic Screening—ethics.
4. Reproductive Techniques—ethics.   5. Sex Preselection.
6. Wrongful Life—ethics. QZ 50 D261g 2009]
RG133.5.D38 2009
362.196′042—dc22
2009009547

9 8 7 6 5 4 3
Printed in the United States of America
on acid-free paper

To my son, Andrew Jesse Jiryu Davis

He who does anything because it is the custom, makes no choice.

John Stuart Mill, *On Liberty*

Acknowledgments

This book owes a great deal to the many friends and colleagues who have taken the time to discuss the issues and to read portions of the manuscript. I am especially grateful to Ingrid Burger, Marion Danis, Rebecca Dresser, Ezekiel Emanuel, Patricia Falk, Joel Finer, Ronald M. Green, Lori Knowles, Paul Lauritzen, Thomas H. Murray, Erik Parens, and Benjamin Wilfond. The librarians at the National Institutes of Health and at Cleveland-Marshall College of Law, especially Laura Ray and Jessica Mathewson, were instrumental in the completion of this book. I am also grateful to Cleveland-Marshall for numerous summer research grants and for the sabbatical leave that allowed me to complete this book, to the Hastings Center for a lovely month spent there as a visiting scholar, and to the Visiting Investigator Program at the National Human Genome Research Institute (NHGRI). NHGRI not only helped fund this endeavor, but allowed me to spend a year among the best group of colleagues one could hope to find.

For the second edition, I am additionally indebted to Dan Egonsson, Suzanne Holland, and Eric Malmqvist, and to all my colleagues at Case Western Reserve University's Center for Genetic Research Ethics and Law, especially Aaron Goldenberg, who taught me all I know about newborn screening. Researchers Alison Boyce, Alexandra Jeanblanc, and, especially, Roselle Ponsaran were indispensable. I thank the Fulbright Senior Specialist Program for an intellectually rich sojourn at Linköping University. This work was partially supported by the Center for Genetic Research Ethics and Law at Case Western Reserve University, through grant #P50-HG-03390 from the NHGRI at the National Institutes of Health.

Contents

Introduction

THIS BOOK IS ABOUT PARENTS AND CHILDREN: children born, not yet born, and not yet even conceived. It is also a book about professionals who get involved in the lives of parents and children, specifically about geneticists, genetic counselors, pediatricians, and other health care professionals who often stand at the intersection between parents, children, and the choices parents face because of the new technologies available to them through genetics and new reproductive technologies.

The concept of choice is at the heart of this book in two ways. First, my thinking on this topic is occasioned by the dramatic array of new choices that has opened up to parents and prospective parents through advances in reproductive technology and in genetics. Let me give just one example. In Chapter 3, I talk of Celia, a woman who is an achondroplasic dwarf. When Celia and her husband (also achondroplasic) married and began their family twenty-five years ago, they had really only one reproductive choice: whether or not

1

to have biological children. The mutation they carried meant that in every pregnancy they had a one in four chance of having a child of average stature, a two in four chance of having a child who was a dwarf like themselves, and a one in four chance of having a child with a double dose of the mutation, which would result in death. Celia didn't want to risk that last possibility, so she made another choice: she and her husband adopted a baby with achondroplasia.

If Celia were starting her family today, she would have a number of choices. She could use ultrasound and amniocentesis to find out the genetic makeup of her fetus in utero, giving her the opportunity to terminate an unwanted pregnancy. The most common way to do this is through amniocentesis, usually performed in the second trimester. A long needle punctures the uterus (while the technician uses ultrasound to watch the fetus, to make sure it is out of harm's way). The needle sucks up a sample of amniotic fluid, the liquid in which the fetus swims. Floating in the amniotic fluid are fetal cells, sloughed off the fetus in much the same way that we continuously slough skin and other cells off our bodies. These cells are then cultured and subjected to genetic analysis, which can tell concerned parents whether their fetus is affected by any number of genetic diseases, including dwarfism. In chorionic villus sampling (CVS) another option, a small piece of placental tissue is removed for analysis; this can be done in the early stages of pregnancy.

Celia could avoid the possibility of abortion by opting for a different choice: in vitro fertilization (IVF) followed by preimplantation genetic diagnosis (PGD). In this technique, Celia's ovaries would be chemically stimulated to produce eggs, which would then be extracted in a minimally invasive procedure. Under local anesthesia, a physician inserts a needle through the woman's vagina and sucks out the mature eggs. The eggs are then put in a petri dish and mixed with sperm from the partner. After a few days, when the fertilized embryos have divided into four or eight cells, they are subjected to genetic analysis. Thus, it is possible to learn the genetic makeup of the embryos before they are even implanted. Embryos that carry the lethal combination of two genes for achondroplasia can be discarded, and Celia and her husband can decide whether to transfer to the uterus embryos that have one copy of the gene and who will be dwarfs like themselves or embryos that will grow up to be children of normal stature.

Sperm donation is another option Celia could choose. By employing the sperm of a nonachondroplasic man through artificial insemination, she could eradicate the chance of having a baby with a double dose of the gene. If she were to go that route, there would still be a fifty-fifty chance in each pregnancy of the fetus being achondroplasic. Celia could combine sperm donation with, for example, IVF and PGD, if she wanted to make sure that her child was of normal stature or to make sure that it had achondroplasia.

So Celia's choices have expanded considerably. Were she beginning parenthood today and depending on which strategies she was willing to employ, she could guarantee a baby of normal stature, guarantee a baby who would be a dwarf, or continue to take her chances with dwarfism while making sure that her baby would not carry the lethal double mutation. She could also, of course, make the same choice that the real Celia did twenty-five years ago and forgo biological parenthood in favor of adopting a child with achondroplasia.

The world in which Celia is making those choices has also changed substantially in the past few decades. Passage of the Americans with Disabilities Act and an increasing sense of power among people with disabilities have arguably widened their choices in areas such as housing, employment, and travel. Some disability rights activists argue that employing techniques to avoid having children who are, for example, deaf, blind, or achondroplasic expresses a lack of respect

3

for the lives of people with those disabilities who are already among us and who may be happy, productive members of society. Adrienne Asch, a scholar who writes on disability issues and who is herself blind, says:

> In a different society than ours, the meaning of the new [reproductive] technologies for people with disabilities could resemble that for people without disabilities. In other words, any special implications for people with disabilities stems primarily, though not exclusively, from their position as the subjects of deep-rooted ambivalence on the part of the nondisabled population.[1]

Asch's point is that much of the "dis" in disability is a result of the way in which society chooses to respond to variations in human functioning. The farsightedness that most of us experience in middle age, for example, is not considered a disability, because it is common and because the means of correction (eyeglasses) are easily available. As our "baby boomer" population continues to age, we shall probably see that more conditions that used to be considered as disabilities are now considered part of the ordinary aging process and accommodation is made without much fuss. Asch concludes that "life with disability can be valuable and valued, and therefore, we must carefully consider the consequences of our disability-prevention activities."[2] The passage of the Genetic Information Nondiscrimination Act (GINA) of 2008 may encourage people with genetically caused impairments, or whose family struggles with genetic risk, to speak out more comfortably about their condition.

One doesn't have to be living with a condition as dramatic as achondroplasia to appreciate the impact that genetic choices have made on our lives. As we shall see in Chapter 5, a new technique for sex selection through sperm sorting is now available. While still imperfect, it allows a couple to influence the sex of their baby before conception (and thus without recourse to abortion). For an outlay of time, money, and hassle, couples can now choose what was once a matter of fate. (Think how different English history would have been had Henry VIII had recourse to this option!) In another example, pregnant women are routinely offered tests such as amniocentesis and ultrasound, which, while looking for signs of trouble, also uncover the sex of the baby. Thus, the pregnant couple now has the choice of getting that information immediately or waiting to be surprised when the baby is born.

This book is also about choice in a second way. I am specifically interested in decisions made by parents that expand or limit the choices that will be available to their children as the latter grow up to be adults themselves. If someone like Celia, for example, makes use of the new available technologies to make sure that her children are achondroplasic like herself, has she severely limited their choices in adulthood, limited them only a little, or simply provided them with a different array of possibilities? And how should we think, in ethical terms, of parents' choices with regard to their children's future lives?

In Chapter 1, I describe the current state of ethical discussion around genetic counseling, particularly from the perspective of counselors themselves. This discussion has been rich and robust, but somewhat unsatisfying in its determined refusal to look beyond the counselor–client encounter to the interests of other persons affected by these decisions.* As the focus of ethical dialogue has broadened

---

* I have used the term counselor throughout the book to refer to any professional who is offering genetic counseling, whether that be a physician, a PhD geneticist, a trained genetics counselor, social worker, or other person. I have referred to the recipients of that counseling as parents, prospective parents, or clients, never as patients, as they are not ill.

from parents seeking to avoid children with severe anomalies to parents seeking to "fine-tune" their progeny's genetic inheritance or to choose for children with a disability such as dwarfism, some of the gaps in the earlier discussion have widened, and it is clear to many commentators that a fresh look at some of these issues is needed. I identify a number of pressure points that call into question the established norms of client autonomy and value-neutral, nondirective counseling. Then I discuss my own perspective, one that brings into focus the autonomy of the child herself, understood as her right to an open future, and gives it an ethical weight of its own. In the chapters that follow, I use the idea of the right to an open future to bring insight to a number of contemporary issues in genetic ethics: testing of children for genetic diseases and carrier status, sex selection, replication of children with the same genetic condition as their parents, and cloning. I have also tackled the newest challenge on the horizon: direct-to-consumer advertising of genetic testing, which will allow people to bypass the gatekeeping function of geneticists, and test themselves and their children largely independent of the medical profession.

Most of the chapters begin with one or two case studies. They are all fictionalized accounts of things that have happened to real people, many garnered from my experiences as a graduate student many years ago at the University of Iowa, where the medical genetics team was kind enough to allow me to dog their heels for a couple of semesters, and from my sabbatical stay at the National Human Genome Research Institute (which is part of the National Institutes of Health). The case studies are all told from the perspective of parents or parents-to-be. But the focus, arguably, is on a child. This child, perhaps not yet born or even conceived, cannot register her opinions or speak her piece, and yet it is she who is center stage in the minds of the parents and professionals I discuss. What are the chances that a child of these parents will be born with a particular condition? How do we understand that condition—as a terrible fate, a serious but manageable disorder, or just a normal human variation? Which of our own values do we bring to the process, and when is that appropriate? For example, in Chapter 1, I describe the Fosters, a Midwest farm couple who have a child with ectodermal dysplasia, a condition that has minor implications for her health and no implications for her intelligence, but which makes her look rather odd. The genetic counseling team was unhappy that they could not provide the Fosters with more information about their genetic risk for having another child with the same syndrome. Without fully articulating their thought process even to themselves, they had assumed that the Fosters would want to avoid a second affected child. But it turned out that they were making unwarranted assumptions; the Fosters were not distressed by their daughter's condition and had little interest in avoiding the birth of future children with the same syndrome. In Chapter 3, I attempt to articulate the values of deaf people who believe that theirs is a rich and viable culture and who look forward to having deaf children, perhaps even in preference to children who hear. In this case, a condition most people would consider a disability is actually prized by a certain group of prospective parents.

In each of the chapters that follows, I want to swing the lens around from a focus on parents to a focus on the experience of the child whose possible birth is the subject of parental decision-making. I want to argue that extreme respect for the autonomy of the parents-to-be, who are the obvious clients of geneticists, has sometimes obscured concern for the autonomy of the child-to-be, who is in an important way also the geneticist's client, or at least the object of her concern.

I have deliberately chosen a group of hard cases. Certainly, my readers won't always agree with me; some of you may never agree with me. I may, at some point in the future, change my own mind about some of these questions. What will not change is the complexity and the importance of the issues before us. With the Human Genome Project completed, scientists are moving ahead into large-scale genome sequencing, to understand genetic variation that cause human disease. As Francis Collins, until recently the Director of the Human Genome Project has written, "The practical consequences of the emergence of this new field are widely apparent. Identification of the genes responsible for human mendelian diseases, once a herculean task requiring large research teams, many years of hard work, and an uncertain outcome, can now be routinely accomplished in a few weeks by a single graduate student...."[3]

The possibilities and the dangers of genetic choice have never been greater. It is crucial that as many people as possible begin to educate themselves about these issues and start to wrestle with the questions they pose.

Making Genetic Choices

Missie is forty-eight years old and pregnant. Two years ago she married Hank, who is fifty. Missie and Hank each had a previous marriage end in divorce, and each had one grown child. They both felt very strongly that their current marriage was "made in heaven," that this was the romance they had been looking for all their lives, and that they wanted to express their love for each other by creating a child. When Missie came to the genetic counseling clinic at Prairie Hospital, she was already in her second trimester. She had been referred to the clinic because a routine ultrasound examination had suggested that there might be a problem with her developing fetus.

At the clinic Missie had another ultrasound, and all the films were looked at by a number of experts. There was agreement that Missie's baby probably had significant anomalies, including myelomeningocele (spina bifida), but the experts could not be absolutely sure. If the baby had spina bifida, the implications could range from death at an early age to partial paralysis. Some people with spina bifida live happy and productive lives, sometimes becoming parents themselves. Others are extremely disabled or mentally retarded, or die early from associated infections.

Missie appeared overwhelmed by the news. She and her husband were blue-collar workers with high school educations and seemed intimidated by the huge teaching hospital in which they found themselves. Missie and Hank expressed pretty clearly that if they were sure that the fetus was damaged, they would opt for an abortion, but they hated the thought that they could be aborting a healthy fetus, especially as Missie's reproductive years were nearly over. Missie kept pressing the genetic counselors to give her a definitive answer as to whether or not her fetus was damaged, but all they could say was, "Probably." Finally she threw up her hands and said, "Okay—I'll do whatever you tell me. Tell me what to do."

The counselors, among themselves, had agreed that it was probably in Missie's best interest to abort. They had a "gut sense" that the fetus was damaged, despite the slight chance that it was healthy. They thought that at their relatively advanced age, Missie and Hank would have an exceptionally hard time with a child who made great demands on their physical stamina. The rural area in which they lived had few support systems in place. Nonetheless, the counselors gently but firmly declined Missie's invitation to tell her what to do. They insisted that she make that decision for herself, with Hank. When Missie said, "Okay, then, let's make an appointment for an abortion," they insisted that the appointment be considered provisional and would be reconfirmed or canceled from home once she had thought about it more.

★ ★ ★

A pediatrician and a genetic counselor, Jim and Janet, both from the genetic counseling clinic at Prairie Hospital, are driving around the state, making home visits. Their first stop is at the Fosters', a farm couple with one three-year-old daughter, Ella, who has ectodermal dysplasia. Because of this syndrome, Ella is rather odd-looking. Her teeth are large and placed almost at random in her mouth. Her thin blond hair looks as though clumps of cotton candy were thrown at her scalp, where they stuck wherever they pleased. But Ella also has regular features, a great smile, and a happy, active attitude toward life. The other consequence of her condition is that Ella has no sweat glands. In the brutal heat of a Midwest summer, she is in danger of heat stroke, since her body cannot cool itself down. The counseling team advises the parents to put Ella in a cool bath if she seems to be overheating, and they arrange for county assistance to install air-conditioning in the farmhouse. They also talk briefly about the availability of cosmetic work on her teeth when she is older.

In the car coming over Jim and Janet had discussed with some concern what they should tell Ella's parents about their risk of having another child with the same syndrome. This condition is not fully understood, and their best guess is that the Fosters have a one in four chance of having another child with that syndrome with every pregnancy. They cannot test for the syndrome prenatally and thus cannot offer the couple the possibility of amniocentesis and prenatal screening. Jim and Janet wish they had more definitive news for the Fosters. They know that the Fosters plan to have more kids, and it frustrates the team that they cannot be more helpful. Cautiously, Jim and Janet raise the issue of genetic risk with the Fosters. To their surprise, the Fosters have only a passing interest in that question. "After all," they say, "Ella is healthy and smart, so why should we be worried about having another child like her?"

IN THE SHORT SKETCH OF CELIA, in the introduction, we already saw a number of different reasons why people might use the services of a genetic counselor. A person might want a diagnosis of her own condition or that of a child. She might know that one or more relatives had a particular condition and wonder what the implications are for herself or her future children. She might want assistance in avoiding a trait or in maximizing the chances that her children will have that condition. Thus, we can see that genetics encompasses just about all of the most emotionally powerful of human experiences: life, death, reproduction, parenthood, and the meaning of health and disease. Not surprisingly, medical geneticists, pediatricians, genetic counselors, and others who work with these issues have devoted much energy to thinking and writing about the ethical issues in genetic counseling.

The profession of genetic counseling is characterized by a respect for patient autonomy that is greater than in almost any other area of medicine. The Code of Ethics of the National Society of Genetic Counselors states that its members strive to

- respect their clients' beliefs, cultural traditions, inclination, circumstances, and feelings;

- enable their clients to make informed independent decisions, free of coercion, by providing or illuminating the necessary facts and clarifying the alternatives and anticipated consequences.[1]

Nowadays most health care codes of ethics speak respectfully of patient autonomy, but outside of genetic counseling, health professionals are still struggling with the challenge of fully respecting the autonomy of their patients. In genetic counseling, however, meticulous concern for client autonomy is the norm. Considering that genetic counseling deals with probabilities (how likely is it that a given baby will have Down syndrome?) and uncertainty (if the baby has Down syndrome, how severely will she be affected?), it is remarkable and laudable that the genetics community has hewed so strongly to an ethic of patient autonomy. In other areas of medicine, physicians at least are very uncomfortable dealing with uncertainty and tend to react by masking it with a false certainty. Jay Katz talks about how doctors will acknowledge uncertainty when discussing scientific problems among their colleagues but mask it—even to themselves—when talking to patients. "They will acknowledge medicine's uncertainty once its presence is forced into conscious awareness, yet at the same time will continue to conduct their practice as if uncertainty did not exist."[2]

The dedication to the ideal of client autonomy in the genetics community can be explained by at least six factors. First, the entire field of genetics is acutely aware of the bad associations of genetics with the eugenics movement so popular in the New World as well as the Old in the first half of the twentieth century, culminating in the horrors of the Nazi era, with its racial stereotyping, destruction of "inferior races," and forced breeding of the Lebensborn project, where unmarried women with the "right" Aryan traits were paired with SS officers and the resulting babies given up for adoption to "good" families. A softer version of this concern is expressed as the fear that new genetic technology will encourage parents to view their children as commodities, as a consumer item one picks and chooses like a new car. Some parents might want to test not only for lethal genes but also for flat stomachs and straight teeth. According to a 1991 Newsweek report, 11 percent of parents in a survey said that they would abort a fetus predisposed to obesity.[3]

A recent development has been an alliance of perspectives from conservative bioethicists on the one hand, and disability rights activists on the other, to warn of a new, "liberal," eugenics. The argument is that where the "old" eugenics involved government coercion to create a "perfect race," the new eugenics is equally intolerant of disability and difference, but is mediated through the individual decisions of prospective parents. Of course, these difficult decisions do not take place in a vacuum. A woman or a couple deciding whether or not to terminate a pregnancy in which the fetus has Down syndrome, is making that decision in a context in which the very fact that the test exists, and that every pregnant woman is advised to test, suggests that society at large believes that Down syndrome is something to be avoided. Further, the degree to which support and resources are available for children with special needs gives a woman more or less freedom to make that decision. Conversely, disability rights activists warn that, if fewer disabled children are born because parents are increasingly intolerant of anything less than perfection, there will in fact be fewer resources available for the babies who are born with disabilities. Disability rights scholar and activist Tom Shakespeare has coined the evocative phrase "retail" versus "wholesale" eugenics to describe this new trend, but unlike many in the disability community, Shakespeare believes that the charge of "eugenics" is unfair. To envision a conspiracy of physicians and scientists intent on eliminating disabled people, is to ignore the degree to which prenatal testing is driven by consumer choice, and also to trivialize women's autonomy and the extent to which women and couples take responsibility for their reproductive choices.[4]

On the other hand, David S. King argues that "the current regime of prenatal testing and genetic selection is eugenic in purpose and outcome." King reminds us that historically government coercion was not "an essential feature" of eugenic theory or practice.[5] Plenty of eugenicists assumed that, once given the facts, most people would want to behave in eugenically "responsible" ways. Today, according to one study, 20 percent of geneticists in English-speaking countries and northern Europe agree that it wrongs society to knowingly give birth to a child with a serious genetic disorder, while in the rest of the world the percentage of geneticists with that point of view rose to much higher levels.[6]

By proclaiming that they have no opinion on what clients ought to do and are merely giving accurate information, geneticists hope to make it clear that they are not the next generation of eugenicists.[7] In fact, the term "genetic counseling" was coined in 1947 by Sheldon Reed to mean "unbiased presentation of information without guidance," in contrast to the earlier terms "genetic advice" and "genetic hygiene." (Ironically, Reed felt that there was little need for guidance, as parents would act "logically" and not have children if they had a high risk of genetic disease.)[8]

The second reason follows on the first: if geneticists are concerned not to be associated with eugenics, they are even more anxious not to be associated with abortion. In our current climate of impassioned debate and political schism over this issue, no physician or counselor wants to be thought of as the person who advises others to have abortions.[9]

A third factor is the lack of available cure or even treatment for many of the diseases that genetics is so good at uncovering. Despite the amazing advances in genetic research in the last two decades, we are still at the point where "We can find almost everything and cure almost nothing." It is the hope of the Human Genome Project and its successors that eventually we will be able to reverse genetic defects and to use gene therapy to treat disorders at their root.[10] Unfortunately, our ability to detect and predict genetic disease precedes by some decades any substantial ability to effect cures. As Nancy Wexler has said:

> Genes are being localized far more rapidly than treatments are being developed for the afflictions they cause,

and the human genome project will accelerate this trend. The acquisition of genetic knowledge is, in short, outpacing the accumulation of therapeutic power—a condition that poses special difficulties for genetic knowing.[11]

If this gap between detection and therapy poses "special difficulties for knowing," it certainly poses special difficulties for advising, and thus encourages a proper humility in genetic counselors who might think they have any special insight into what prospective parents ought to do with the knowledge genetics affords.

The fourth factor encouraging client autonomy is the intensely personal nature of the decisions being made: whether to have children at all, to have children with this potential mate, to use contraception, to resort to abortion, and so on. These are the types of decisions around which our society traditionally throws a strong shield of privacy and deference. They are also issues that attract a great deal of feminist interest and concern. It was feminists, for example, who led the fight for access to contraception and who insisted on having a say in such matters as to how childbirth would be "managed." As the overwhelming majority of genetic counselors at present are women, it is not surprising that they bring a high degree of feminist sensitivity and respect for client decision making to these issues.

A fifth factor is the way in which genetic decisions can have major consequences for entire families.[12] As one counselor said, "I am not going to be taking that baby home—they will."[13]

Finally, as the field of genetic counseling has matured, it has defined itself as a therapeutic encounter as well as an educational one. The understanding of that encounter is heavily indebted to the pioneering psychotherapist Carl Rogers and his ideal of client-centered, nondirective counseling, and thus to an ethos of client empowerment.[14] The difficulties of nondirectiveness, and the intense commitment to that value, are poignantly expressed by one counselor who said, "I am aware that I can do a very subtle thing and make a decision for somebody, and I really work at not doing that—it's really terrible, it's not appropriate."[15]

This commitment to client autonomy is expressed in the twin tenets of value-neutrality (a decision's moral worth is determined solely by whether it is the right decision for that client) and nondirectiveness (the counselor won't try to influence clients or tell them what to do). The ethos of value-neutrality finds expression in the practice of nondirective counseling. Counselors define their task as giving accurate information to clients in such a way that clients can use that information to act according to their own values. To quote Francis Collins, director of the National Human Genome Research Institute until 2008, and thus of the Human Genome Project:

> It should be explicitly stated . . . that one of the prime tenets of genetic counseling is patient autonomy. Counselors do not seek to tell patients whether they should obtain certain information or what they should do with it if they acquire it. The goal is to inform patients about what is possible and what their options are. Counselors help patients to work through those options and then to decide on their own principles what is the right choice for them.[16]

Critiques of Genetic Counseling Ethics

The Ambiguity of Choice

Although within the field of genetic counseling the commitment to client autonomy remains largely unshaken, it has also been the focus of some criticism. One type of criticism points out that while genetic testing is usually presented in terms of increased choice for women especially and prospective parents generally, in fact it may also represent a lessening of choice. Making choices is an emotionally exhausting and energy-consuming endeavor, as anyone who has helped a high school student through agonizing college choices knows well. The more possibilities exist, the more it appears necessary to defend and argue for one's choice. Tibor Scitovsky illustrates this difficulty using a homely analogy:

> If, beginning with a situation in which only one kind of shirt were available, a man was transposed to another in which ten different kinds were offered to him, including the old kind, he could of course continue to buy the old kind of shirt. But it does not follow that, if he elects to do this, he is no worse off in the new situation. In the first place, he is aware that he is now rejecting nine different kinds of shirts whose qualities he has not compared. The decision to ignore the other nine shirts is itself a cost, and inasmuch as additional shirts continue to come on the market, and some are withdrawn, he is being subjected to a continual process of decision-making even though he is able, and willing, to buy the same shirt. In the second place, unless he is impervious to fashion, he will feel increasingly uncomfortable in the old shirt.[17]

For the woman who strongly wishes to avoid having children with disabilities, who is not opposed to abortion for this reason, who has medical insurance and good access to quality care, and who is comfortable with a high-tech pregnancy, the advent of genetic testing may well be liberating. A woman who heretofore might have been afraid to conceive after forty because of the relatively high risk of Down syndrome and other diseases, or the couple who are both carriers for Tay-Sachs disease and might have had no children at all rather than risk tragedy, may find that genetic testing allows them increased control over their lives, increased abilities to predict reproductive outcomes, and more reproductive choices. But for the woman who would not contemplate abortion, or for whom Down syndrome is one acceptable (if not desirable) outcome of pregnancy, the existence of this technology can be oppressive. Women speak of the "rituals" and routines of genetic testing within pregnancy,[18] and of the real difficulty they experience in fighting the momentum of those routines and assumptions if they decide that testing is not right for them.[19] Now that the choice exists whether or not to have a baby with, for example, Down syndrome, the decision to go ahead and have that baby may actually be much harder to make. Indeed, as testing becomes more and more routine, the disease being tested for becomes ever more dreaded, ever more unthinkable.[20]

Another way in which genetic testing may actually curtail choice is in the unspoken but powerful assumption that parents will react to the news of fetal abnormality by having an abortion. As Abby Lippman points out, the search for and rapid acceptance of earlier forms of prenatal diagnosis reinforces the assumption that, of course, the reason to diagnose is to be able to abort, and the earlier the abortion the better.[21] There is even concern that as genetic abnormalities come to be seen as avoidable mistakes rather than "the luck of the draw," society may be less willing to pay for the education and support of people with genetic problems. Health maintanance organizations (HMOs) and employers may give people a choice: test and abort, or bear the consequences yourself.[22] In a study of British obstetricians, 13 percent agreed with the statement "The state should not be expected to pay for the specialized care of a child with a severe handicap where the parents had declined the offer of prenatal testing."[23]

In my own mind I can discern a subtle shift in the way in which I view people with certain anomalies. Twenty years ago, seeing a woman in the supermarket with a child who has Down syndrome, my immediate reactions were sympathy and a sense that that woman could be me. Now that testing for Down syndrome is virtually universal in the United States, when I see such a mother and child I am more likely to wonder why she didn't get tested. Theresa Marteau and Harriet Drake conducted a study in three European countries to determine how the birth of a child with Down syndrome is "explained." They found that "[w]omen who decline the offer of testing are seen as having more control over this outcome, and are attributed more blame for it, than are women who have not been offered tests and also give birth to a child with Down syndrome."[24]

Choice is constrained if the social supports necessary for raising a child with the genetic disease are not available. Parents whose fetuses test positive for cystic fibrosis or phenylketonuria (PKU) do not have real choices if society does not offer assistance with the treatments necessary to cope with those diseases, such as the expensive special diet required to protect children with PKU from mental retardation.[25]

Another problem is the scarcity of genetic counselors to help people understand increasingly complex choices. As more and more conditions are understood to be at least partially genetic in origin, the need for genetic counselors grows exponentially, and the supply has certainly not kept up. For example, the web site Alzheimer's Mirror has genetic counselors on staff to provide telephone counseling to people who have chosen to be tested for a genetic pattern that, depending on the results, might confer a lessened, average, or greater risk for developing Alzheimer Disease. As someone who recently went through that testing as part of a research protocol, and had more than one face-to-face session with a genetic counselor, I know that this is a very complicated area. It took me two sessions and a number of phone calls before I really understood the statistical basis of the risk assessment they gave me, and what, if anything, it meant for my life. I find it difficult to believe that telephone counseling is an adequate substitute.

Making Room for the Best Interests of the Child

The second type of critique focuses on the possible good that could be done or harm that could be averted if geneticists were more willing to act on their own considered values, either in counseling patients or in setting limits on how they will enable genetic expertise to be used. From this perspective, it might be considered a good thing if a geneticist challenged the values of a couple who wanted to use amniocentesis and abortion for sex selection (in the absence of a sex-linked disorder), as we will see in the case of the couple in Chapter 5. Or perhaps a geneticist, faced with a couple who declared that they "could not possibly cope" with a child who had cystic fibrosis (CF), might insist that they meet at least one family with a CF child before deciding to abort.

Arthur Caplan has been a vocal critic of what he calls the Dragnet or "just-the-facts, ma'am" approach to genetic counseling. Caplan's critique rests in part on counseling's "powerlessness" in the face of "what may be immoral requests," such as the desire to have a deaf child, which we will look at in Chapter 3. Further, Caplan argues that the enormous potential of genetic medicine makes it imperative that geneticists drop the facade of value-neutrality in order to confront the questions of what counts as disease or disorder, what kinds of disorders ought to be targeted for detection and treatment, and how to set research priorities for gene detection (and, I would add, for gene therapy).[26] In fact, as we shall see in Chapter 3, the desire of some people with disabilities to attempt to ensure that they have only children who share that disability, for example, people with achondroplasia, like Celia, or deaf people who are proud of their culture and want to make sure that they have deaf children, has become a lightning rod for this recent critique of nondirective genetic counseling.

Imagine such a deaf couple approaching a genetic counselor. Their goals are to learn more about the cause(s) of their own deafness and, if possible, to maximize the chance that any pregnancy on which they embark will result in a deaf child. As Walter Nance described the challenge, writing in 1993:

> It turns out that some deaf couples...would actually pre-fer to have a deaf child. The knowledge that we will soon acquire [due to the Human Genome Project] will...pro-vide us with the technology that could be used to assist such couples in achieving their goals. This, in turn, could lead to the ultimate test of nondirective counseling. Does adherence to the concept of nondirective counseling actu-ally require that we assist such a couple in terminating a pregnancy with a hearing child or is this nonsense?[27]

The genetic counselor who adheres strictly to the tenets of value-neutral, nondirective counseling will respond to this couple by help-ing them to explore the ways in which they can achieve their goal: a deaf baby. In the few years since Nance described this scenario, we have even developed the technology to select for a deaf baby without the necessity of aborting a hearing fetus. This couple could produce a number of embryos through in vitro fertilization (IVF), have these embryos analyzed in the first days of life by a technique we call pre-implantation genetic diagnosis (PGD), and then transfer to the wife's uterus only those embryos with the genetic mutation for deafness. (Of course, some people would consider this ethically tantamount to abortion, as it still involves the destruction of a human embryo.) But as Nance's depiction of this scenario suggests, the counselor may well feel extremely uneasy about her role here. It is one thing to sup-port a couple's decision to take their chances and "let nature take its course," but to treat as a goal what is commonly thought of as a risk may be more pressure than the value-neutral ethos can bear.

Robert Wachbroit and David Wasserman offer a helpful but only partial answer to this dilemma in distinguishing value-neutrality from nondirectiveness. The goal of nondirectiveness is patient autonomy. Value-neutrality, they point out, is valued primarily because it appears to be a necessary condition for patient autonomy, the unstated assumption being that the open expression of the counselor's values undermines clients' ability to make their own decisions. Wachbroit and Wasserman challenge that assumption, arguing that clients are not that fragile, and also that unspoken social biases may be more threatening to autonomy than those that are clearly put on the table.[28]

Mary Terrell White relies on the notion of social responsibility and the work of theologian H. Richard Niebuhr to make some parallel arguments.[29] White claims that the client-autonomy-centered perspective of genetic counseling is "lopsided," because it neglects the extent to which human actions are predicated on social relationships. She wants genetic counselors to engage in a more energetic dialogue with their clients, remaining attentive to the counselors' responsibility to "promote socially responsible use of their services," and to serve as "gatekeepers for genetic services." White's approach has some serious problems. For one, I think she misconstrues the autonomy-based approach of genetic counseling as being purely informational, tending to slight emotional and psychosocial issues. In fact, most genetic counseling encounters are extremely attuned to family and social issues. For people struggling with a genetic trait that has already adversely affected one or more family members, images of "family" are at the forefront of the discussion. For example, people with one child affected by a disease such as cystic fibrosis often worry that having another affected child will compromise their ability to care for the first one. From my own experience observing seminars for genetic counselors and hearing them critique their interactions with clients, I think they are almost too attuned to the therapeutic side of counseling, seeming to feel that they have not done their jobs if their clients fail to exhibit intense emotional affect during a session.

White agrees that "clients must be free to make their own decisions and even their own mistakes"; her proposal is aimed at improving "the quality of the counseling process, not the outcome." Thus, neither White nor Wasserman and Wachbroit fully address the problem. If a couple approached a counselor looking not only for information but for practical assistance in creating a deaf child, the counselor might not be satisfied with a solution in which she expressed her moral reservations and then went on to help them anyway. What Nance and Caplan seek, and I think White as well, is a principled argument on which to base a refusal for assistance. This refusal need not rise to a legal prohibition, as there are many good reasons for keeping government surveillance out of the delicate process of genetic counseling, but it could become part of the ethical norms and standards of care of those professions that engage in genetic counseling. In the remainder of this chapter I put forth such a principled argument, based on the idea of a child's right to an open future.

The Child's Right to an Open Future

As we saw, when moral challenges arise in the clinical practice of genetics, they tend to be understood as conflicts between the obligation to respect client autonomy and other ethical norms, such as doing good and avoiding harm. Sometimes the harm to be avoided is to another family member, as when a person who has tested positive as a carrier for Tay-Sachs disease refuses to share that information with siblings and other relatives, despite the clear benefits to them of having that knowledge, or when a family member declines to participate in a testing protocol necessary to help other members discover their genetic status.

This way of looking at moral issues in genetics often leaves counselors and commentators frustrated, as White's essay illustrates. By elevating respect for client autonomy above all other values, it may be difficult to give proper weight to other factors, such as human suffering and the just allocation of resources. Also, by privileging client autonomy and by defining the client as the person or couple who has come for counseling, there seems no space in which to give proper attention to the moral claims of the future child who is the endpoint of many counseling interactions.

To describe the problem primarily as one that pits beneficence (concern for the child's quality of life) against autonomy (concern for the clients' right to make their own decisions about these matters) makes for obvious difficulties and frustrations. These are two very different values, and comparing and weighing them invites the proverbial analogy of apples and oranges, or as a friend of mine says, "apples and bookcases." In fact, the perennial critique of a principle-based ethics is that it offers few guideliness for ordering principles when duties conflict.[30] Beneficence and respect for autonomy are values that will always remain in some tension within the field of genetics and genetic counseling. For all the reasons I listed above, counselors are committed to some version of nondirective counseling. But surely most or all of them are drawn to the field because they want to help people avoid or at least mitigate suffering. This is increasingly true as training programs in genetic counseling shift the practice from a research model to a social work model.[31]

As an ethicist, I have reasons for not pursuing the conflicting-values approach. For one thing, as will become clear as this chapter goes on, I have strong commitments to the primacy of the value of autonomy. I think that the reasons geneticists embrace client autonomy are mostly valid, and I am in no hurry to attempt to persuade them away from it. Further, to the extent that these issues end up in the public arena and become topics of public discourse, I want respect for individual rights to remain as strong a component of that discourse as possible. Thus, faced with the ethical challenges of our new genetic capabilities, I suggest a different way to look at these problems. I propose that, rather than conceptualizing them as a conflict between autonomy and beneficence, we recast them as conflicts between parental autonomy and the child's potential autonomy, what philosopher Joel Feinberg has called "the child's right to an open future." [32]

Feinberg begins his discussion of children's rights by noticing that rights can ordinarily be divided into four kinds. First, there are rights that adults and children have in common (the right not to be killed, for example). Second, there are rights that are generally held only by children (or by "child-like" adults). These "dependency-rights," as Feinberg calls them, derive from the child's dependence on others for such basics as food, shelter, and protection. Third, there are rights that can be exercised only by adults (or at least by children approaching adulthood), for example, the right to choose and to practice one's religion. Finally, there are rights that Feinberg calls "rights-in-trust," rights that are to be "saved for the child until he is an adult." [33] These rights can be violated by adults now, in ways that cut off the possibility that the child, when she or he achieves adulthood, can exercise them. A striking example is the right to reproduce. A young child cannot physically exercise that right and a teenager might lack the legal or moral grounds on which to assert such a right, but clearly the child, when she or he attains adulthood, will have that right. Therefore the child now has the right not to be sterilized, so that the child might exercise the right to reproduce in the future. Rights in this category include virtually all the important rights we believe adults have but which must be protected now to be exercised later. As John Locke says, "Thus we are born free, as we are born rational; not that we have actually the exercise of either; age that brings one, brings with it the other too."[34] Grouped together, these rights constitute what Feinberg calls "the child's right to an open future."

Feinberg illustrates this concept with two contemporary examples. The less controversial one, and the one more familiar to readers of bioethics, is the Jehovah's Witness child who needs a blood transfusion to save his life, but whose parents object on religious grounds. In this case, the parents' right to act upon their religious beliefs and to raise their family within the religion of their choice conflicts with the child's right to live to adulthood and to make his own life-or-death decisions: As the Supreme Court said in a nonmedical case involving Jehovah's Witnesses:

> Parents may be free to become martyrs themselves. But it does not follow, that they are free in identical circumstances to make martyrs of their children before they have reached the age of full and legal discretion when they can make that decision for themselves.[35]

Thus, Feinberg argues that the parents' religious rights must give way before the child's right to life, and the right to grow to adulthood to make his or her own choices.

The second example is more difficult. I will dwell on it at length because it is helpful to have a model for thinking about parental control over children's lives that does not involve some of the issues related to disability with which I will be dealting in later chapters.

In 1972, in a famous United States Supreme Court case, *Wisconsin v. Yoder*, a group of Old Order Amish argued that they should be exempt from Wisconsin's requirement that all children attend school until they are sixteen or graduate from high school.[36] The Amish, of course, did not have to send their children to public school; they were free to create a private school of their own liking. (They could also have set up a home-schooling system that met state curricular requirements.) But they chose to frame the issue in the most stark manner: to send their children to any school past eighth grade would be antithetical to their religion and their way of life, and might even result in the death of their culture.

The case was framed as a freedom-of-religion claim, on the one hand, and the state's right to insist on an educated citizenry, on the other. Within that framework, the Amish won. First, they were able to persuade the Court that sending their children to school after the eighth grade would potentially destroy their community

> [b]ecause it takes them away from their community, phys-
> ically and emotionally, during the crucial and formative
> adolescent period of life. During this period, the children
> must acquire Amish attitudes favoring manual work and
> self-reliance and the specific skills needed to perform the
> adult role of an Amish farmer or housewife. In the Amish
> belief higher learning tends to develop values they reject
> as influences that alienate man from God.[37]

Second, the Amish convinced the Court that the state's concerns that children be prepared to participate in the political and economic life of the state did not apply in this case. The Court listened favorably to expert witnesses who explained that the Amish system of home-based vocational training—learning from one's parents—worked well for that community, that the community itself was prosperous, and that few Amish were likely to end up unemployed. The Court said:

> The value of all education must be assessed in terms of its
> capacity to prepare the child for life. It is one thing to say
> that compulsory education for a year or two beyond the
> eighth grade may be necessary when its goal is the prepa-
> ration of the child for life in modern society as the major-
> ity live, but it is quite another if the goal of education

[can] be viewed as the preparation of the child for life in the separated agrarian community that is the keystone of the Amish faith.[38]

What only a few justices saw was that the children themselves were largely ignored in this argument. The Amish wanted to preserve their way of life. The State of Wisconsin wanted to make sure that its citizens could vote wisely and make a living. By claiming that leaving school after the eighth grade is not significantly different from leaving at age sixteen, the justices ducked the question of whether the liberal democratic state owes all its citizens, especially children, a right to a basic education that can serve as a building block if the child decides later in life that she wishes to become an astronaut or a playwright, or perhaps to join the army.[39] As we constantly hear from politicians and educators, without a high school diploma one's future is virtually closed. By denying them a high school education or its equivalent, parents are virtually ensuring that their children will remain housewives and farmers. As the Court said, the children are being "prepar[ed]...for life in the separated agrarian community." Even if the children agree, is that a choice parents ought to be allowed to make for them?

Feinberg's critique of the Court's decision lies in his argument that every child has a right to an open future and that severe limitations on that right, even by the child's parents, ought not to be allowed. In this case, Feinberg and some of the justices felt that the difference between leaving school after eighth grade and at age sixteen (only two more grades for many children) was not enough to justify the state in putting such a heavy burden on the Amish parents' religious beliefs. My own instincts go in the other direction. If Wisconsin had good reasons for settling on high school graduation or age sixteen as the legal minimum to which children are entitled, then the Amish children were entitled to that minimum as well, despite their parents' objections. Perhaps I am wrong in my pessimism about the children's capacity to reverse that decision when they become adults, by getting more education and finding employment outside the Amish community, but that is just a pragmatic, factual disagreement between me and Feinberg. Our theoretical point is the same: parents ought not to make decisions about their children that severely and irreversibly restrict their right to an open future.

Feinberg makes his point in the context of a legal argument and uses legal cases to make his arguments. Thus, his conclusions are couched in terms of whether or not the state ought to step in to prevent parents from foreclosing their children's futures, for example, by forcing parents to send their kids to school or to allow their kids to have life-saving blood transfusions. In this book I am interested primarily in ethical rather than legal arguments, and I am not calling for new laws regulating the practice of genetic counseling, genetic diagnosis, and assisted reproductive techniques, with an eye to protecting the child's right to an open future. I believe that the process of genetic counseling and its attendant activities is so delicate that to insert the state into that interaction would be like inviting a bull into a china shop. However, it is possible to call for policies and attitudes—for example, at the level of professional societies and training—that reflect the ethical stance for which I argue. For example, as we shall see in Chapter 4, a number of professional groups have promulgated policies against genetic testing of children for adult-onset disorders. Finally, I do think it is worthwhile to at least examine a different system, and therefore in Chapter 3 I will describe the policy-making role of the Human Fertilization and Embryology Authority (HFEA) in the United Kingdom, and have posed some questions about whether such a process might be useful on this side of the Atlantic.

The right to an open future is, of course, something that can be argued only within the context of a liberal state. Liberalism, as Lainie

Friedman Ross asserts, is "a political theory of limited government that provides institutional guarantees of personal liberties and basic rights for its adult members. Adults are free to devise and implement their own life plans. This includes the freedom to form and raise a family according to their own conception of the good." But, as Ross admits, "less clear-cut is how liberalism deals with children."[40] Parental autonomy, the "freedom to form and raise a family according to their own conception of the good," can often conflict with the future autonomy of children to "implement their own life plans" when they become adults. For example, if adults were able to betroth their children in marriage in ways the children could not undo when they reached adulthood, they would be interfering with their children's right to a basic tenet of adult autonomy: the right to choose whether and whom they will marry. Such betrothal is illegal in this country and, I think, ought to be rejected on ethical grounds as well, no matter how sympathetic we might be to the parents' motivations in trying to arrange for their children's future well-being, and no matter how accepted such betrothal might be in the parents' culture of origin. This example, along with the example of the Amish and education, highlights a deep conflict between two different concepts of liberalism: commitment to autonomy and commitment to diversity. William Galston argues:

> A standard liberal view (or hope) is that these two principles go together and complement one another: the exercise of autonomy yields diversity, while the fact of diversity protects and nourishes autonomy. By contrast, my... view is that these principles do not always, perhaps even do not usually, cohere; that in practice they point in quite different directions in currently disputed areas such as education.... Specifically, the decision to throw state power behind the promotion of individual autonomy can weaken or undermine individuals and groups that do not

and cannot organize their affairs in accordance with that principle without undermining the deepest sources of their identity.[41]

Galston claims that, "properly understood, liberalism is about the protection of diversity, not the valorization of choice.... To place an ideal of autonomous choice...at the core of liberalism is in fact to narrow the range of possibilities available within liberal societies."[42] In other words, to require that the Amish support their children's ability to make autonomous choices when they become adults is to require that the Amish not be fully Amish.

How should a liberal—one devoted to the principle of individual autonomy—react to Galston's challenge? Because, as Galston says, we cannot have it all, both unbridled diversity and unbridled choice, I support the side of individual autonomous choice. Choosing the basic signposts of one's life is one of the indicia of what philosopher Martha Nussbaum calls "a good human life...at which societies should aim for their citizens."[43] Of the ten "functional capabilities" that Nussbaum lists for this minimal good human life, number six is "Being able to form a conception of the good and to engage in critical reflection about the planning of one's own life. This includes, today, being able to seek employment outside the home and to participate in political life."[44] Number ten is "Being able to live one's own life and nobody else's. This means having certain guarantees of non-interference with certain choices that are especially personal and definitive of selfhood, such as choices regarding marriage, childrearing, sexual expression, speech, and employment."[45]

A nineteenth-century philosopher who would have agreed enthusiastically with Nussbaum is John Stuart Mill. In *On Liberty* he claims that the very measure of a human being is the extent to which he makes life choices for himself, free of societal pressure:

> The human faculties of perception, judgment, discriminative feeling, mental activity, and even moral preference, are exercised only in making a choice. He who does anything because it is the custom, makes no choice.[46]

Mill would abhor a situation such as that of the Amish communities in *Yoder*, which unabashedly want to give their children as few choices as possible. But, on the other hand, it is clear from both common sense and from Mill's own statements that in order for people to have choices about the patterns of their lives (and to be inspired to create new patterns), there must be more than one type of community available to them. To quote Mill again: "There is no reason that all human existence should be constructed on some one or some small number of patterns."[47] As we look at the past three centuries of American history, we see what an important role different community "patterns" have played, from the Shakers to the Mormons to Bronson Alcott's Fruitlands to the communal experiments of the 1960s. If those patterns are to exhibit the full range of human endeavor and experiment, they must include communities that are distinctly antiliberal. Not only does the panoply of widely different communities enrich our culture, but it also provides a welcome for those who do not fit into the mainstream. As Mill says, "A man cannot get a coat or a pair of shoes to fit him unless they are either made to his measure, or he has a whole warehouseful to choose from: and is it easier to fit him with a life than with a coat[?]"[48] Some of us are geniuses who make our lives to "fit our measure," and others are happy to fit into the mainstream, but for yet others, the availability of a "warehouseful" of choices increases the possibility of a good fit. And for some, a good fit means an authoritarian community based on tradition, where one is freed from the necessity of making choices. Galston is correct in pointing to the paradox: if the goal of a liberal democracy is actively to promote something like the greatest number of choices for the greatest number of people, this seems to entail hostility toward narrow-choice communities such as the Amish. But if the Amish, because of that hostility, fail to flourish, there will be fewer choices available to all.

The compromise I promote is that, as members and supporters of a liberal state, we should tolerate even those communities most unsympathetic to the liberal value of individual choice. However, this tolerance must exist within a limiting context, which is the right of individuals to choose which communities they wish to join and to leave if they have a mind to. Even Galston begins with the presumption that society must "defend...the liberty not to be coerced into, or trapped within, ways of life. Accordingly, the state must safeguard the ability of individuals to shift allegiances and cross boundaries." [49] Thus, I believe that the autonomy of the individual is ethically prior to the autonomy of the group. Both ideals have powerful claims on us, but when group rights would extinguish the abilities of individuals within them to make their own life choices, then liberals ought to support the individual against the group (using the force of law in extreme cases). This is especially crucial when the individual at issue is a child, who is particularly vulnerable to adult coercion and therefore has special claims on our protection.

In the same way, I believe that the autonomy of the individual is ethically prior to the autonomy of the family, even though, chronologically and developmentally, it is certainly the other way around where children are concerned. And again, where the family exercise of its rights to "form and raise a family according to [its] own conception of the good," as Ross puts it, threatens to extinguish the abilities of children to choose their own lives when they become adults, I believe that the family behaves wrongly and that liberals ought to support the (future) rights of the children at issue. (Again, in extreme cases, this will require the force of law, as when families deny their

children basic education or medical care, but the topics I will discuss
in this book do not necessarily lend themselves to legal solutions.)
Unfortunately, it is precisely where children are concerned that
groups are understandably most jealous of their prerogatives to guide
and to make decisions. The Amish are an example of a group guarding its ability to shape the lives of its children; deaf parents wishing
to ensure deaf children are an example of families pursuing the same
goals. Of course, communities and families ought to—in fact, they
must—strive to shape the values and lives of the children in their
care. Not to do so would lead to social and individual pathology.
But when that shaping takes the form of a radically narrow range of
choices available to the child when she grows up—when it impinges
substantially and irrevocably on the child's right to an open future—
then I maintain that liberalism requires us to intervene to support
the child's future ability to make her own choices about which of the
many diverse visions of life she wishes to embrace.

Genetic Choices, Parental Investment, and the Right to an Open Future

In subsequent chapters, we will look at parental choices made possible by the "new" genetics. Many writers use the trivializing and
dismissive term "designer babies," as if women were making choices
analogous to choosing a handbag or a new winter coat. This not
only predetermines the course of the conversation, but it is disre-
spectful to the motivations that go into parental choice, even choices
that I believe are misguided. I prefer the more neutral term *directed
procreation*. Parents can, for example, choose the sex of their baby.
Parents in families with hereditary deafness can avoid having deaf
children, or decide to have deaf children. In the not-too-distant
future, parents will probably be able to choose "enhancements" that

might range from perfect pitch to at least some of the characteristics that have made Michael Phelps the ultimate Olympic swimmer. (I thought it was interesting that the television commentators kept referring to Phelps's size 14 feet as "flippers.") We will analyze these choices through the lens of the child's right to an open future.

The most common objection made to my arguments is that it is part of human nature to have strong expectations for our children's futures. Ronald M. Green reminds us that many parents have very specific expectations of their children and "frequently do all they can to impose their wishes on children"; he points to the many toddlers one sees at alumni events wearing "diminutive Dartmouth sweatshirts inscribed with their hoped-for graduation years."[50] Green agrees with philosopher William Ruddick that parents "beget, bear, and raise children to fulfill certain aims, sometimes eccentric or personal."[51] In other words, we should not single out directed procreation as bearing unique risks to the child's future autonomy, but tolerate it to the same extent that we tolerate parochial schooling, Dartmouth sweatshirts, and pink flowered wallpaper for baby girls.

In response, I agree that parents do often have strong expectations that children will join the family business, attend the mother's school, or be "a chip off the old block" in any number of ways. That is not necessarily a reason to encourage easy access to genetic and reproductive techniques that sharpen and increase this tendency. Rather, the startling aspects of directed procreation could be a "wake-up call" for a more considered critique of our current childrearing practices, everything from cosmetic orthodontia to building a college admissions resume from the time one is a toddler. "Bioengineering gives us reason to question the low-tech, high-pressure child-rearing practices we commonly accept."[52] But more important, I believe that directed procreation has the alchemy to turn a hope into a virtual entitlement. At present a couple can hope that they will have a boy with the requisite physique to play football for their alma mater, but even the most obsessed parents realize that they embark on each pregnancy knowing that the chances of having a boy are roughly fifty-fifty, not to mention the chances of having a child with the talent, build, and interest to play football. But if those parents pay large sums of money, and make a huge investment in time, effort and personal hassle (including temporarily railroading their sex life) in order to make sure that the child is a boy, or to clone a successful football player, they are likely to feel *entitled* to the desired result, or at the very least will find it significantly more difficult to take their direction from the child as to whether football coaching or music camp is the best way to spend the summer. Instead of parents dressing their toddler in a $20 sweatshirt advertising the child's future enrollment at Dartmouth, imagine if a parent were able to put down a $50,000 nonrefundable deposit on a child's place in the Dartmouth freshman class. How open would that parent be to the child's attending Juilliard instead or forgoing college entirely in favor of hitch-hiking around the world? And yet, $50,000 is small peanuts to what many people already pay for directed procreation.

Thus, I argue that it is a qualitatively different thing, for example, to be born a girl as a result of chance (even to parents who had been hoping for a girl) than to be born a girl as a result of sex selection. What is important for the future of the child is not so much the nature of the trait selected as the expectations that motivate the parents to select it. This has important implications for the moral permissibility of the selection. Even traits (such as intelligence) that are in themselves useful for all life plans may be chosen with very particular life plans in view, with expectations that may restrict the child's future freedom.[53] Being chosen as a girl through sex selection, involving a huge investment in time, money, and personal inconvenience, will too often, I fear, give the parent a sense of entitlement to whatever girl-like qualities the parent was hoping for, or to feeling cheated if the child does not fulfill those expectations. (Notice that these qualities do not have to be stereotypical. Feminist parents might well want a girl in order to groom her to be the first female President.) Rosamond Scott misses an important point when she writes that:

> If...we think simply about the interests of the future children who might be selected on the grounds of their sex, if parents do have particular ideas about girls or boys, then when they have either a boy or a girl *without* sex selection, they are very likely in any event to raise a child according to these ideas....If the child they happen to have is not seriously harmed by these presumptions—and it seems inherently unlikely that it would be harmed—then we can also say that sex selection itself would not risk serious harm to another child selected according to its sex.[54]

What Scott ignores is the quality of investment and therefore entitlement, that parents are likely to feel, once they have gone through the substantial rigors and sacrifice of directed procreation for sex selection.

Green makes the same mistake when he says that "genetic choice does not seem so different from the various forms of socialization that parents undertake."[55] Green argues that, although genetic choices may "seem to be more hard-wired and less easily set aside than the lessons and experiences that parents provide," a child can use his enhanced capabilities for very different goals than the ones the parents had in mind. "I may dream that my son or daughter will become an astronaut, but the child may choose to apply the given analytical skills to a business career."[56] Green is correct that some forms of "socialization" are comparable in effect to the expense and rigors of directed procreation. A parent who rises at 4 a.m. six mornings a week for five years to supervise his child's swim lessons, or who moves the whole family to another state, perhaps causing the parents to live apart from one another, in order to support a child's talent at ballet, may well be making sacrifices and investments that equal those of directed procreation. One hopes that such a parent is following the child's lead, and one hopes that the parent accepts with grace the child's decision to take a different path. Directed procreation is like moving to Arizona, installing a tennis court at great expense, and signing up for nonrefundable lessons with the country's best tennis coach, all before conception.

To get a sense of the magnitude of the investment, let us take a quick overview of how directed procreation is accomplished. I am going to ignore trait selection by abortion as inimical to most people's ethical intuitions, at least in the West (excluding the practice of abortion to avoid having a child with serious impairment or disease).[57]

Methods of Directed Procreation

Sperm Sorting

The least technically complex method of directed procreation is sperm sorting, which is discussed at greater length in Chapter 5. Although this method is useful only for sex selection, it has the advantage of working before conception, so there are no concerns about the moral status and ethical disposition of human embryos. Sperm sorting, trademarked as MicroSort, is offered exclusively by the Genetics and IVF Institute (GIVF), in Virginia and California. Exploiting the fact that X-bearing sperm have more deoxyribonucleic acid (DNA) than Y-bearing sperm, MicroSort uses flow cytometric separation technology to separate out the desired sperm, which is then used for intrauterine insemination or IVF. The process is far from perfect; MicroSort technology currently provides an average increase in X-bearing sperm to 88 percent in the enriched X-sorted sample and an increase of Y-bearing sperm to an average of 73 percent.[58] This is significantly higher than the roughly fifty–fifty ratio in natural procreation, and perhaps it is reassuring to note that parents embarking on MicroSort must know that there is a substantial likelihood that they will end up with a child of the less preferred sex.

The cheapest cost per cycle is $3,765 (excluding travel and accommodations, of course). This assumes that the woman is monitoring her ovulation herself. With full monitoring at the MicroSort clinic, the cost jumps to $5,415 per cycle. This is for sorting, monitoring, and intrauterine insemination, and does not include fertility drugs, IVF, or other collateral costs depending on how MicroSort is used in conjunction with other technologies. MicroSort reports its pregnancy rate at 15.6 percent per cycle. Patients are urged to use barrier methods of birth control while having intercourse during a MicroSort cycle.

According to the Patient Information Packet,[59] some patients use Clomid (Clomiphene Citrate), a fertility drug, to stimulate follicles in order to make it more likely that the cycle will result in a pregnancy. MicroSort does not publish statistics on how many of its clients use follicle stimulating drugs, but when I visited GIVF in 1999, it was presented as a routine part of the process. Medical risk associated with the use of fertility drugs is still the subject of debate. Clomid can cause ovarian hyperstimulation syndrome (OHSS), which in rare cases can be life-threatening.[60]

In Vitro Fertilization and Preimplantation Genetic Diagnosis

Preimplantation genetic diagnosis (PGD) piggybacks on the opportunities presented by in vitro fertilization (IVF). Originally developed to detect and avoid serious genetic conditions such as Tay-Sachs Disease, PGD can also be used for other purposes, including sex selection. "[V]irtually any of the hundreds of genetic tests now commercially available, and the many more in development, could be used to test embryos."[61]

IVF and PGD begins with the woman taking fertility drugs, and having the ripe eggs removed through a minor surgical procedure involving sedation and local anesthesia. After a number of embryos are created in the lab through IVF, one or two cells from each embryo are carefully removed and analyzed for the relevant trait(s). Most embryos seem to tolerate this procedure unharmed, although there is a small risk of increased abnormalities,[62] and embryos with the desired traits are then implanted in the uterus or frozen for subsequent use. A successful pregnancy using IVF usually takes more than one cycle. Risks to the resulting babies are not completely known; risks to the mother include ectopic pregnancy and OHSS.[63] IVF on its own costs about $10,000–$12,000 per cycle, with no guarantee of a successful pregnancy. The addition of PGD can add $2,500–$4,000.[64] Embryo biopsy negatively affects the implantation rate of embryos;[65] in other words, couples using IVF for infertility decrease their chances of success if they add on PGD in order to choose a genetic trait.

In sum, every currently available method of trait selection with any serious promise of success, comes at an extremely high price. The only exception would be parents who already have a need for IVF and PGD to avoid a serious disease, and who, having discarded affected embryos, are left with a large number of equally healthy embryos about which they also have "incidental" knowledge of other traits. At that point, since only some embryos will be selected for the first attempt at implantation, there seems little harm in choosing on the basis of traits such as sex, or perhaps, in the next few years, perfect pitch.

Here is the question for the future: Is directed procreation ethically problematic only because a massive parental investment bodes ill for the open futures of children thus conceived? What if future research allows us to choose girls or boys in a simple, inexpensive way that interferes little with sexual intercourse? We could imagine a vaginal spermicide that would be hostile only to x- or y-bearing sperm, or some food supplement a man could eat that would cause him to produce only one or the other. If producing a girl or boy child becomes almost as easy as in the old folk beliefs—hanging one's overalls on one or the other side of the bed, sliding a knife beneath the pillow—would there still be cause for concern about parental constraint of the child's future autonomy? If choosing a child's genetic traits is as simple as designing the Mini Cooper I recently ordered from England, need we still worry about parental entitlement?

I think not. As committed as I continue to be in my opposition to directed procreation that threatens a child's right to an open future, I must concede that my concerns are not ontological but contingent on the practical factors that make up parental investment.

For those who share Michael Sandel's concerns about "the moral status of nature, and the proper stance of human beings towards the given world," [66] or fear that any trait selection automatically "commodifies" or "instrumentalizes" [67] the child (more than parents always to some extent commodify children), the extent of investment will probably play a small role in their thinking. I do not share these romanticized concerns; I am more pragmatic. The more investment of time, money, travel, inconvenience, physical discomfort, and medical risk a parent puts into directed procreation, the more I fear a parent who feels entitled to the desired result. That parent, I fear, will be less than supportive of the child's open future. As market forces and medical research make such investments relatively trivial, the less I fear that effect. The President's Commission on Bioethics, in a 2003 report on "Biotechnology and the Pursuit of Happiness," wrote:

> The salient fact about human procreation in its natural context is that children are not *made* but *begotten*. By this

we mean that children are the issue of our love, not the product of our wills. A man and a woman do not produce or choose a *particular* child, as they might buy a particular brand of soap; rather, they stand in relation to their child as recipients of a gift.[68]

In contrast to the Commission's perspective, if choosing the sex or any other trait of one's children *were* as simple and inexpensive as choosing a bar of soap, I would be much less worried.

There will, of course, always be new technological manipulations on the horizon, as unimaginable today as IVF was unimaginable to all but the science fiction writers in the years before the birth of Louise Brown in 1978. These new manipulations, if they are likely to be burdensome in any number of ways, will give rise to new concerns about parental investment, as some old manipulations become cheaper and simpler. The key is to keep our eye, not only on the quality of the desired traits themselves, but on how many sacrifices parents must make to achieve them.

Deliberately creating a child who will be forced irreversibly into the parents' notion of the good life violates the Kantian principle of treating each person as an end in herself and never as a means only.[69] All parenthood exists as a balance between fulfillment of parental hopes and values and the individual flowering of the actual child in his or her own direction. The decision to have a child is never made for the sake of the child, for no child then exists. We choose to have children for myriad reasons, but before the child is conceived, those reasons can only be self-regarding. The child is a means to our ends: a certain kind of joy and pride, continuing the family name, and fulfillment of religious and societal expectations among others. But morally the child is first and foremost an end in herself. Good parenthood requires a balance between having a child for our own sakes and being open to the moral reality that the child will exist for her own sake, with her own talents and weaknesses, propensities and interests, and with her own life to make. In William Ruddick's evocative phrase, parents are both "guardians and gardeners."[70] Parental practices that close exits virtually forever are insufficiently attentive to the child as an end in herself. By closing off the child's right to an open future, they define the child as an entity who exists to fulfill parental hopes and dreams, not her own.

A Short Discussion
of Harm

2

BECAUSE DISCUSSIONS OF GENETICS and of reproductive technology often involve cases of children who are not yet conceived or born, ethical discussions in this area have to negotiate a pitfall that I will call the harm conundrum. Other writers have called it the problem of wrongful life[1] or the wrongful-handicap problem.[2] The essence of the problem is that often parents are criticized (or defended against criticism) for bringing into the world a child who is physically or mentally damaged in some way that seems very likely to cause that child a degree of suffering greater than that of normal children. But some writers argue that this criticism is misplaced because, counter to our intuitions, no one has actually been harmed, as the child herself could not have existed otherwise than in her suboptimal state. Thus, unless the child's current existence is so terrible that she would have been better off never having been born, she has not been harmed by being born in her damaged state.

Let me clarify this with a hypothetical example. Imagine a couple who are told by their doctor that if they conceive in the month of May, they will have a high likelihood of conceiving a child who would lack one hand, whereas if they waited until June, their risk of conceiving a child with a birth defect would be no greater than that of the general population. The couple went ahead and conceived in May when they could just as easily have waited the extra month, and as a result had a child, Tim, with only one hand.[3] I think most of us (if we knew the full story) would be highly critical of this couple. And yet who is harmed? Tim is not harmed because had he not been born with one hand, he would not have been born at all. Had his parents waited the extra month, they would have had a different, probably nondamaged child, but it would not have been Tim. It is not as if there were ever the choice between having a damaged Tim and an undamaged Tim. So, unless we want to say that life with only one hand is worse than no life at all, Tim himself has no cause for complaint and has not been harmed.*

---

* By the same token, it makes little sense to say that Tim has the "right" to be born with two hands. As in Kant's famous dictum, *ought* implies *can*, and there is simply no way that Tim could have been born other than the way he was. Thus when Feinberg speaks of a child's right to an open future in reference to Amish children being denied an education, the use of the term *right* makes sense, as the same child could have access to schooling or be denied it. In most of the topics that I discuss in subsequent chapters, involving preconception decisions such as sex selection, the use of the term *right* becomes somewhat metaphorical. If, for example, little Jane is born as a result of her parents' use of sperm sorting to ensure that they have a girl, and if, as I argue in Chapter 5, that is morally problematic because it compromises Jane's right to a future that is relatively unconstrained by intense gender expectations, I can only mean that metaphorically. If Jane's parents took my advice and had a child without sex selection, that child (even if a girl) would almost certainly not be Jane.

To draw this discussion closer to the real issue of parents who wish to have deaf children, the topic of our next chapter, imagine a couple, Carl and Karla, each of whom is deaf. Carl is deaf because his mother was exposed to German measles while she was pregnant; Karla is deaf due to a genetic condition. This is a dominant condition; therefore in each pregnancy Karla has a 50/50 chance of having a deaf child. Knowing the odds, Carl and Karla decide to conceive and to take their chances. Some people might criticize their decision, especially if they actually have a deaf child. One argument against them would be that they ought not to burden society with the extra needs of a deaf child if the situation could be avoided. This argument is easy to refute, as deaf people are fully capable of becoming productive members of society. If they have a child who is severely retarded, or doomed to a very early and protracted death, as in Tay-Sachs disease, the argument on behalf of society would be less easy to counter. Most ethicists are loath to make that argument too strongly because it smacks of eugenics and hints at the frightening possibility of the state attempting to legislate under what conditions people can have children.

But what about the second kind of argument, that for this couple to have a deaf child is wrong for the sake of the child itself? As John Robertson asserts[4] and others agree,[5] this kind of claim can be sustained only in very horrible instances, because it relies on the assertion that the child's life will be so terrible that it would have been better off if it had not been born. Remember that this particular child—call her Carol—could either be born deaf or not exist at all. Deafness was an intrinsic part of her deoxyribonucleic acid (DNA). Had her parents taken steps to avoid a deaf child, they would have had a different child altogether, not Carol. (Thinking about this is reminiscent of that common obsession of children: "Who would I be if my parents hadn't met?") There may be perspectives from which we can argue that Carl and Karla's laissez-faire approach was morally wrong, but we cannot claim to be arguing that from Carol's perspective (unless we are prepared to claim that being deaf is literally a fate worse than nonexistence). As Robertson says, "From the child's perspective, the risk-creating activity is welcome, since there is no alternative way for this child to be born."[6]

For clarity's sake, imagine another instance: a couple who are deaf for nongenetic reasons (e.g., childhood illness). This couple, of course, has no more likelihood than the general population of giving birth to a deaf child. If they want to increase their chances of having a deaf child, they will have to deliberately expose the fetus to some teratogen such as German measles. In this case, it is easier to show that the child—call her Ann—has been harmed. Baby Ann had two possibilities: being born hearing or being born deaf. Her parents deliberately did something to ensure the latter condition. If being deaf is less desirable than being able to hear (and this is something we will address at length in Chapter 3), then Ann has been harmed.

Now imagine a third scenario. Again we have Carl and Karla. For unrelated reasons, this couple needs to make use of in vitro fertilization (IVF) to conceive a child. Like most couples using IVF, they try to produce a number of embryos, of which only some will be implanted. They decide to use preimplantation diagnosis (in which cells are removed from the eight-celled embryos on the third day after fertilization and subjected to DNA analysis, without harming the original embryos) and transfer to the uterus only those embryos that carry the gene for deafness. In the petri dish, simplifying the situation somewhat, we see four embryos: A, B, C, and D. Embryos C and D have the dominant gene for deafness; the others do not. Carl and Karla choose to transfer only embryo C, who emerges nine months later as Carol, a healthy, deaf baby. Has Carol been harmed? As in the first scenario, Carol had only two possibilities: to be born deaf or not to have been born at all. It seems hard to argue that Carol has been harmed in this instance, for the same reasons that she had not been harmed in the first scenario, where her birth was a matter of chance. And yet this is the scenario that so troubles Walter Nance[7] and that Arthur Caplan cites as an example of an "immoral" use of genetic counseling.[8] If the harm here is not to Carol and not to society, who or what has been harmed?

Bioethicist John Harris insists that there is no moral difference between choosing a deaf embryo through preimplantation genetic diagnosis (PGD), and refusing an available cure to a newborn deaf baby. Nor does he see a moral difference between choosing to have a deaf child through PGD and deliberately deafening a child.[9] Matti Hayry, however, argues that there is an important ethical difference, even though the "impersonal outcome" is the same. In both instances, a deaf individual exists, and the outcome was foreseen when the choice was made. But when a more "personal or individualistic" angle is incorporated, Hayry believes that the two scenarios are quite different.[10] If prospective parents deliberately deafen a fetus or child, then an individual is now deaf who otherwise would have existed as the same individual, but with hearing intact. Whereas, if the deaf embryo had not been selected, that individual would not have existed. "Put simply, parents who select a deaf embryo (or any embryo for that matter) *give that specific potential person a chance to live*, with the qualities that that individual happens to have. By contrast, parents who deafen a hearing child...*change the qualities of an already existing individual*."[11]

Most commentators seem to agree that there is no purely logical way out of what Dan Brock calls the wrongful-handicap conundrum. In the case of a child whose life is arguably not worth living, one can say that life itself is a cruelty to the child. An example might be a child with the autosomal recessive disease, Hallopeau-Siemens syndrome. In this rare disease that manifests at birth, the skin literally comes off if the baby is touched, leaving painful scar tissue. The infant must be fed by tube, but the top layers of mucous membranes inside his/her mouth and esophagus fall away at each feeding. In the "best" situation, the child would live as long as ten years, and then die of skin cancer.[12] But when a child is born in less than ideal circumstances or is partially disabled in ways that do not make for a life of horrendous suffering, there seems no way to argue that the child himself has been harmed. This may appear to entail the conclusion, counter to our common moral sense, that therefore no harm has been done. "A wrong action must be bad for someone, but [a] choice to create [a] child with its handicap is bad for no one."[13]

A partial solution is to begin with the uncontroversial statement that each person, other things being equal, ought to seek to maximize goods (such as happiness) or at the very least to minimize harms (such as pain and suffering). This works in some instances. It allows us, for example, to criticize Tim's parents. By simply waiting another month to conceive, they could have had a child who probably would have experienced less suffering in his/her life than will Tim. Thus, harm has been done, even though one cannot attach it to a specific entity, such as Tim.

However, this beneficence-maximizing approach can take us only so far. In Tim's case, it was easy to see that no one *gained* happiness from Tim's missing hand, and also that being born with two hands is preferable (despite all the inspiring ways in which young Tim might grow up to overcome his handicap). In the case of baby Carol, however, where the parents made a deliberate choice that having a deaf baby is preferable, not only do we have to come to grips with the question of whether being able to hear is better than being deaf (which we will take up in Chapter 3), but we also have to balance the satisfaction Carl and Karla feel in raising a deaf child like themselves against the frustration and limitations experienced by Carol. In other scenarios we will take up in later chapters, the prospective parents' choice may be the only way in which they will be able to reproduce. If we are asking about possible harms to the child who is born through cloning, and if cloning is the only way in which this couple is able to reproduce, then we must try to weigh the possible harm experienced by a child as a result of being a clone, which we will address in Chapter 6, against the suffering of this couple if they remain (biologically) childless. But we cannot weigh the experience of a cloned child against the experience of an uncloned child whom they otherwise could have produced, because having an uncloned child is not an option for this couple. Thus, a weighted beneficence approach will take us only so far.**

One major reason why this debate has proved so difficult—or, to put it another way, why so many people of commonsense end up pushed into counterintuitive corners—is that it has been couched largely in legal terms, even when specific essays are supposedly about ethical rather than legal implications. Many of the articles in this debate use legal terms such as "wrongful life" to frame the discussion, or rely heavily on court cases. In part this may be due to the strong influence of law professor John Robertson. Robertson's argument on most innovative reproductive technologies goes something like this: Procreative liberty is constitutionally protected, and therefore

---

** An astute reader will notice that I am deliberately avoiding terms such as *utilitarian*. This is because, at some level, all reasonable ethical theories take doing good and avoiding harm (i.e., beneficence and nonmaleficence) as important principles. The primary difference between utilitarian theories and others is that the former take this goal to be the only relevant criterion for ethical evaluation. For a good overview of ethical theory in bioethics, see Beauchamp, Tom L. and James, F. "Childress," *Principles of Biomedical Ethics,* 4th ed. (New York: Oxford University Press, 1994).

can be limited by the state only when its exercise places a substantial burden on others. Unavoidable harm to the children expected to result from an innovative reproductive technology ("noncoital conception") certainly qualifies as a reason for the state to limit procreative liberty if the harm is likely to be substantial. But as the only way this child could be born at all would be through this new technology, in order for the child to be harmed, it must be put in a state so bad that nonexistence would be preferable. "From the perspective of the offspring, alienation, genetic bewilderment, even a physical handicap, is preferable to no existence when the damage and birth of the child is unavoidable. Unavoidable prenatal injury so severe as to constitute, from the child's perspective, 'wrongful life' is highly unlikely with noncoital conception."[14] But the result of Robertson's argument is quite narrow: that the state cannot "prohibit private sector use of these techniques."[15] Notice how little ground this covers: Robertson does not claim that the state has to enable people to use this technology, through financial or other support, nor does he claim that scientists ought to put their energies into this area, or that health professionals should cooperate with people wishing to use it. He argues merely that it cannot be criminalized. Except for cloning, and perhaps use of abortion for sex selection, outright prohibition on assisted reproductive technologies has never been a serious issue in the United States.

Robertson's analysis has little to say about the allocation of financial resources, participation of health professionals, or ethical evaluation of the various uses of assisted reproductive technologies. It is also totally dependent on a specifically American jurisprudence of constitutional protection of procreative liberty. And yet, in part because he himself tends to fudge the line between ethical and legal discourse, he is often taken to be making larger ethical claims than he really is. For example, in contiguous sentences Robertson says,

"Transferring embryos [created through noncoital techniques] and thus risking damaged offspring in such cases cannot be condemned on grounds of protection of offspring, because transferred embryos have no alternative way to be born without risk of damage," and, "The offspring have no grounds for wrongful life suits against their parents or the physicians involved, because the damage was unavoidable."[16] The first sentence certainly sounds as though it is meant to be an ethical argument, but the second sentence retreats to narrower ground—the likelihood of a successful tort claim. There is a huge difference between "condemning" an action on moral terms, and having grounds for a successful lawsuit, but Robertson often seems to be conflating the two.

Because the language and thinking in this discussion have been so influenced by the tort theory of wrongful life, let me say a little bit about that. Tort law—the law of injuries—is part of our civil, as opposed to criminal, law. Tort law is a way to compensate people who have been injured and to deter potential tortfeasors by making it expensive to act in ways that put others at unreasonable risk of harm. Tort law is not about pointing fingers; the law scrupulously talks about "liability" rather than "guilt." A person found liable can be assessed damages to be paid to the injured party but cannot be put in jail, lose her driver's license, or be forced to pay a fine to the state. In a criminal action, the state itself brings a case against the accused. Even if the victim didn't want to bring charges or was beyond compensation, the state could still proceed, because it is the community itself that is hurt by someone's criminal behavior, as well as the specific victim (which is why there can be such a thing as a "victimless crime"). If the state succeeds in its case, the lawbreaker may go to jail or pay a fine, but that doesn't help pay the victim's bills. A civil action, by contrast, is brought by the victim (or his proxy or heir), and if he wins, the compensation is paid to him. Thus, if there is no victim, no person who has been harmed by the act in question, there can be no tort claim.

We can now see why it is extremely difficult, virtually impossible, to bring a successful tort case for wrongful life, the tort of causing someone to be born. There are other, somewhat related cases that are often confused with this. For example, if parents give birth to a child with Down syndrome due to professional negligence (e.g., mixing up amniocentesis results), the parents can successfully sue for wrongful birth (if they can convince a jury that they otherwise would have terminated the pregnancy). And parents in some states can win suits for wrongful pregnancy if they conceive a child through someone's negligence (e.g., the pharmacist dispenses aspirin instead of birth control pills) even if the resulting baby is healthy. The argument is that had they not had the child, they would have been better off financially. Many states will compensate parents for wrongful pregnancy to the extent of compensation for a narrow range of expenses, such as maternity clothes, labor and delivery fees, and time lost from work; a few will allow parents to be compensated for the education and maintenance costs of the child for eighteen years.[17] But it is almost impossible for a child to win a wrongful life suit, in which he attempts to show the court that he himself has been injured by being born at all. Courts are squeamish about putting a dollar value on such a metaphysical claim. As one judge said, "[T]he choice is between a worldly existence or none at all. To recognize a right not to be born is to enter an arena in which no one could find his way."[18] Courts also fear that acknowledging wrongful life claims would send a message that the lives of handicapped people are not worth living, and would "stir the passions of jurors about the nature and value of life, the fear of non-existence, and about abortion."[19] The costs of the child's special educational and medical needs can be handled through the parents' successful wrongful birth suit. When wrongful life suits have prevailed, it is usually because there is no other way to make sure that the child will be adequately supported into his adult life and that his special educational and medical needs will be met, but compensation for the actual pain and suffering of his injured existence is not accepted.[20] This emphasis on the identifiable victim, which is inextricably part of the very nature of a tort claim, has had an unfortunate effect on the ethical discussion.

Another unfortunate element imported from tort law is the notion that the harm at issue must somehow be quantifiable. We can see why this is so, because the goal of the tort system is to compensate victims, to attempt as far as possible to "make them whole." Compensation brings with it an inevitable element of comparison between the plaintiff's situation before the tort and her situation afterward. If before the tort you had a house, and as a result of the tort your house burned down, the remedy is obvious: pay you the value of the house (and compensate you for the hassle and time spent in rebuilding it). In medical cases this becomes somewhat more problematic; paying someone's medical bills plus time lost from work for a broken arm makes sense, but it is harder to compensate him for the pain and inconvenience. Clearly, there are many cases where the logic of tort seems to run out altogether, as when people are rendered infertile, or when a loved one is killed. In those cases, tort law probably exists more as a deterrence than as a remedy. In all these cases, however difficult they may be, the action is always grounded on the notion of a comparison between ex post and ex ante states. But as Ronald M. Green points out, "[h]arms can occur without someone being made worse off than they were before ... there are forms of conduct we are unwilling to tolerate that do not make people worse off in the strict sense."[21] In other words, Green argues, correctly in my view, that the requirement of tort law that there be an identifiable victim with a "reduced post ante status" is not universally true in law or in ethics.[22]

A number of philosophers interested in applied ethics have tried to get around the harm conundrum, with varying degrees of success. Dan Brock is the most successful, in my opinion, because he explicitly turns away from the focus on "the special moral complaint" the handicapped child has against its mother.[23] Instead Brock begins with the principle that "[i]t is morally good to act in a way that results in less suffering and less limited opportunity in the world."[24] A parent violates that principle if, due to her negligence, her child loses a hand to blood poisoning, for example. But she also violates that principle if, through her negligence, she conceives a child with one hand when she could almost as easily have conceived a child without that disability. The fact that in the second case we speak of two different children does not change the immoral quality of her act. Brock acknowledges that "one apparent difficulty" with his argument is that it does not explain our "commonsense moral judgment" that the mother in the second case has actually wronged the one-handed boy.[25] But, outside of a court of law, I am not sure that anything important hinges on that.

The other philosophers grappling with this problem all rely in some way on rejecting the idea that a successful wrongful-life claim must rest on a comparison between the child's present state and his hypothetical state as a nonborn being. As Joel Feinberg explains: "[T]he grounds for charging that a wrongdoer has violated another's right not to be born do not include reference to a strange never-never land from which phantom beings are dragged struggling and kicking into their mothers' wombs and thence into existence as persons in the real world. Talk of a 'right not to be born' is a compendious way of referring to the plausible moral requirement that no child be brought into the world unless certain very minimal conditions of wellbeing are assured."[26]

Expanding on this idea, Bonnie Steinbock says:

> The escape from this dilemma is to see that it is not nec-
> essary to maintain that the child would be better off
> never having been born in order to claim that he or she
> has been wronged by birth. Instead, we can say that it is a
> wrong to the child to be born with such serious handicaps
> that many very basic interests are doomed in advance,
> preventing the child from having the minimally decent
> existence to which all citizens are entitled. While this is
> something less than a right to be born a whole functional
> human being, it is not dependent on the implausible view
> that a life with serious impairments is always worse than
> no life at all.[27]

Cynthia B. Cohen points out that Robertson and Feinberg make
a mistake when they conflate nonexistence before life and nonexistence after having lived. In her view, it requires a much greater
degree of suffering to say of someone, "He would be better off
dead," than to say, "It would be better if he had never been conceived." "Death," says Cohen, "has characteristics that lead us to
evaluate it as bad, whereas preconception nonexistence strikes us as
neither good nor bad."[28]

This leads Cohen to add that:

> The interests of children who might be born of the new
> reproductive technologies are not adequately captured by
> the "wrongful life" standard. The comparison that par-
> ents and physicians must make when they assess whether
> use of these technologies would negatively affect the good
> of children who might result is not between *death* and the
> condition of these children were they to be born with
> certain deficits. If pre-conception nonexistence, unlike
> death, is neither good nor bad, then any life that would
> be worse than it will *not have to be as bad as the life of devas-
> tating deficits set out in the wrongful life standard.* A life with

serious, but not devastating deficits, could be bad and therefore worse than preconception nonexistence, which is neither good nor bad.[29]

Green rejects the "impossible task" of trying to compare existence with nonexistence and instead compares the child's actual state with "the reasonably expected health status of others in the child's birth cohort."[30] He argues that preconception lives are "fungible, interchangeable generic units." "Parents intending to have a child do not imagine the identifiable child Mary whom they come to know in the years following her birth, but a 'generic' child with qualities like those of most other children being born in its cohort." When the real child emerges and takes its place in the "slot" waiting for it (e.g., "the Smith family's third child"), the parents compare the state of this child against the "imagined child" they had in mind when they decided to go ahead with parenthood in the first place.[31] Similarly, the child itself, as it grows, compares its life with that of the "other lives it might reasonably be thought to have lived in its family and time."[32] This reasoning leads Green to assert that: "In the absence of adequate justifying reasons, a child is morally wronged when he/she is knowingly, deliberately, or negligently brought into being with a health status likely to result in significantly greater disability or suffering, or significantly reduced life options relative to the other children with whom he/she will grow up."[33]

I am not persuaded by Green's reasoning, although I think he and Cohen are correct to warn us against equating the harm of nonexistence, which is really no harm at all, with the harm of death. To my way of thinking, at least for our purposes here, Brock's approach is best, because it reflects our universal moral intuition that to avoid suffering is a good thing and therefore that persons who, whether deliberately or out of negligence, bring into the world children in a less than optimal state when they could easily have done otherwise have committed a moral wrong. I do think we are stuck with a paradox: when little Tim is born with only one hand, harm has been done, but not to Tim. But to allow this paradox—this "philosophism," in Leon Kass's term—to short-circuit our ethical reasoning would be absurd.[34] Our common moral intuitions speak strongly against that conclusion. For one example, among those who believe in family planning at all, it is common for people to delay the birth of their next child until the time is reasonably optimal. To say, "I will allow myself to become pregnant now, even though our house is infused with asbestos, both parents are out of work, and the first two kids are still in diapers, because, after all, whatever child I have in these conditions would be better off than had it not been born at all," is an obviously goofy conclusion. As the National Bioethics Advisory Commission concluded when putting aside the wrongful life conundrum, the metaphysical argument is "problematic" and can lead to "absurd conclusions."[35]

Further, I believe that would-be parents have an obligation to make reasonable efforts to give their prospective children as good a life as possible. This is a special obligation growing from their role as parents, over and above the obligation all persons have to act in ways that minimize suffering. This is what it means to be a decent parent. Thus, if parents know that child A conceived in May will probably have only one hand, while child B conceived in June will probably be born intact, they have an obligation as parents to not conceive in May. This obligation exists despite the fact that child A, were she to be conceived and born, would enjoy her life even with only one hand, and despite the fact that she would have no *logical* cause to reproach her parents.

In the chapters that follow, I have focused on the harm done to children when parents significantly limit the range of choices open to them when they become adults, whether that limitation is due to a physical disability or due to intensified parental expectations engendered by parents' ability to use technology to create children with specific desired traits, such as gender. Thus, in Chapter 3, I argue that genetic counselors should not assist deaf parents seeking to ensure that they have deaf children, because being deaf significantly limits the child's future options and is thus a harm to the child. In Chapter 5, I show why preconception sex selection may harm the children who are born through that strategy, because it concretizes parental gender expectations and thus makes it difficult for the children to escape gender stereotypes. In the final chapter, I argue against cloning when done for a certain category of reasons, again because I believe that the practice has the potential seriously to limit the autonomy of the children born in that manner. I hope that in this chapter I have addressed and neutralized the wrongful-life conundrum, at least to the extent that we can get on with the substantive business of scrutinizing the ethical issues.

Choosing for Disability

3

Recently I met Celia, a vibrant woman in her fifties who has achondroplasia. Celia is about four feet tall and had to hoist herself into the chair provided for her at the front of the room. She is well educated and articulate, full of salty humor, and obviously enjoying a full and satisfying life. Much of Celia's life seems to revolve around her condition, but in a positive way. In her late teens, she volunteered for one of the first genetic studies of achondroplasia being conducted at Johns Hopkins University. Through that study, she met her husband, also achondroplasic. She also became employed at Johns Hopkins in their genetics department, first as a clerk but eventually as clinic coordinator. As the only adult achondroplasic on the premises when parents would come for genetic counseling, or with their babies, and be told the news, she ended up doing a lot of ad hoc counseling as well, telling people what her life was like with the condition. Celia is very involved with the Little People of America (LPA), taking a leadership role in its activities, a role that has involved her in international travel.

In some ways one could almost wonder if Celia's "disability" has not resulted in a wider life than she otherwise would have had. She described growing up in a large, close-knit family in which all her aunts, uncles, and cousins lived within a few blocks of each other in Baltimore. Her father, she said, viewed anything outside of Baltimore as alien territory; Virginia, Celia's husband's home state, was like "Ethiopia" to Celia's father. She is the only one of her siblings to leave Baltimore, and she said impishly that she's not sure her father ever forgave her.

When Celia and her husband had been married for a few years, they decided to start a family. However, at that time it was not possible to test fetuses for the achondroplasia gene. A double dose of the gene (a one out of four chance in every pregnancy) is always fatal, an outcome Celia had wanted to avoid at all costs. She also said quite frankly that she had wanted to avoid having a child of average stature. The solution was to adopt an achondroplasic baby.

I asked Celia to speak more about their reluctance to have a child of average stature, and also to comment on the experience of her achondroplasic friends who had average-size children. She spoke at length of the physical context of her world, in which she and her husband, and other couples like them, had cut down the legs of chairs, designed kitchens with only low cabinets, and in general made their circumstances fit their needs. She talked of how reluctant she would be to change that, and how an average-size child might not fit in. She also spoke about how hard it would be to carry and care for a child who at age five was as big as its parents. She spoke poignantly of the need she felt every child has to "look up to" its parents and to feel safe and protected by them physically, and how a child of average stature would not have that experience. *She worried that an average-size child with "little" parents would feel embarrassed at school (she seemed to take in stride the social problems an achondroplasic child would experience). Finally, she mentioned how important LPA was in her life, and how her son had practically grown up in LPA.*

If Celia were beginning her family now, she and her husband would probably approach a genetics counselor for assistance in ensuring that they had a child with achondroplasia, possibly by using in vitro fertilization and preimplantation genetic diagnosis to retain only embryos carrying one copy of the relevant gene.

★★★

Marta and Geoff are both deaf. They always describe themselves as Deaf, using the capital letter D, to signal their pride in being deaf and their rejection of the idea that their nonhearing state is a disability. Marta is the only deaf person in her family, and her parents had a hard time adjusting to life with their deaf daughter. Eventually Marta's parents learned some American Sign Language (ASL or Sign), but they never proved fluent, and only one of Marta's siblings can sign. Geoff, on the other hand, is a child of two deaf parents, and his one sibling is deaf too. Geoff began to sign at the same age at which hearing children begin to say words. Geoff's whole family, including his maternal grandparents, all sign fluently and are part of a larger deaf community. They attend a deaf church and play in a deaf bowling league. Marta and Geoff met at Gallaudet University, the only institution of higher education for the deaf in America. They married in their senior year, moved to a small Midwestern city, and now, in their late twenties, are thinking of starting a family.

Marta and Geoff recently learned about connexin 26, a newly discovered genetic mutation that is responsible for about half of all

GENETIC DILEMMAS

> *nonsyndromic genetic deafness.[1] They approach the genetic counseling clinic in their area with the following idea. They will both be tested to ascertain if their deafness is due to the connexin 26 mutation. If they both have the mutation, then they will have at least a one in four chance with each pregnancy of having a deaf child. But rather than leave it to chance, they will use in vitro fertilization and preimplantation genetic diagnosis to transfer to the uterus only deaf embryos. They know that this will make it harder to conceive (and also cost a lot more), but they feel strongly that they want to raise only deaf children.*

IN THIS CHAPTER I take up one of the thorniest issues in genetic ethics—how should professionals respond to parents who wish to use the new techniques of reproductive and genetic medicine to make sure that their children's genetic heritage reflects their parents' disability? Is this another example of client autonomy, where professionals should be delighted that new techniques allow them to give clients what they want? Or should professionals decline to participate in ventures that aim at producing children who are intentionally less than healthy? And what do we mean by "healthy," anyway?

Because most of the literature on this topic has revolved around the issue of deaf couples, I will focus on deafness for most of this chapter, and return to the example of dwarfism only at the end.

Is Being Deaf a Harm?

At first glance, it might appear a silly question to ask whether being deaf is a harm. Ethically, we would certainly include destroying someone's hearing as being a "harm"; legally, one could undoubtedly receive compensation if one were rendered deaf due to someone else's negligence. Many deaf people, however, have recently been arguing that deafness is not a disability at all, but a linguistic and cultural identity. As Bonnie Poitras Tucker (a deaf law professor) explains it:

> During the past decade, a growing concept of Deaf culture has taken root. Under this concept, people who cannot hear are viewed as either deaf (with a small d) or Deaf (with a capital D). Persons who view themselves as deaf are those who, although impaired in their ability to hear, have assimilated into hearing society and do not view themselves as members of a separate culture. People who call themselves "Deaf," however, view and define deafness as a cultural identity rather than as a disability for some purposes; they insist that their culture and separate identity must be nourished and maintained.[2]

In the Deaf President Now movement at Gallaudet University in March 1988, students shutdown the university and refused to allow a newly appointed president to take office, because the trustees had once again chosen a hearing president for a deaf university. The significance of that moment has often been compared to that of the Stonewall riots in gay and lesbian American history. Looking at photographs taken during those tumultuous weeks, it is clear that the Gallaudet students regarded themselves as one more oppressed minority, not as a disabled group. One huge banner declared—*We Still Have a Dream*; another placard said—*Jews, Catholics, Women, Blacks: Now It's Time for Deaf.*[3] The issue was revisited in 2006, when the trustees appointed Jane Fernandes as president. Fernandes was deaf, but "not deaf enough." She was not fluent in ASL, and lacked some of the other indicia that deaf "insiders" associate with being authentically deaf, such as physical warmth and directness, and "a certain attitude, both amused and cynical, toward the hearing world that results from a shared set of experiences." The resistance to Fernandes (who eventually stepped down) showed that the simple biological fact of being deaf was not enough—a whole set of cultural traits were in play as well. Ironically, the hostility to Fernandes was in part because deaf culture is weakening, diluted by the internet, the decline of residential schools for the deaf, and the demise of deaf social clubs. Gallaudet is thus the last bastion of deaf culture, heightening the importance of the choice of leader.[4]

Increasingly, deaf people have been asserting their claims not merely to equal access (e.g., through increased technology), but also to equal respect as a cultural minority. As one (hearing) reporter noted:

> So strong is the feeling of cultural solidarity that many deaf parents cheer on discovering that their baby is deaf. Pondering such a scene, a hearing person can experience a kind of vertigo. The surprise is not simply the unfamiliarity of the views; it is that, as in a surrealist painting, jarring notions are presented as if they were commonplace.[5]

From this perspective, abortion of deaf fetuses is considered genocide. That same word is also used to describe the use of cochlear implants, permanent surgical hearing aids that enable deaf children to hear (although the extent of their success varies widely and is itself a subject of controversy) and which the medical community considers a highly desirable intervention.[6] Unlike hearing aids, which amplify sound and deliver it to the external part of the ear, cochlear implants actually receive and process sound and, bypassing the injured part of the ear, deliver sound information directly to the brain. The device includes a small component that is surgically implanted in the inner ear, and an external component that looks like a regular hearing aid and which in turn is linked to a pocket-size speech processor.[7]

Cochlear implants are much more efficacious when used for people who became deaf after they had acquired at least some language. The most successful user would be an adult or adolescent who had only recently been deafened. As one's common sense would expect, acquiring language is harder than recovering it.[8] However, if the implants are used in young children, it appears that the earlier the children are fitted with the implants—for example, when it is first discovered that they have a hearing disability—the better, as that enables them to acquire language as early as possible. Thus, parents of children who are born deaf or who are prelingually deafened must make a crucial choice for their children before they can expect any input from the children themselves: should they raise the children as deaf, with Sign as their primary language tool, or should they embrace cochlear implants as a "deliverance" from the disability of deafness?

In 1990, the Food and Drug Administration approved the use of cochlear implants for deaf children ages two through seventeen, thereby setting off a "bitter and emotional debate" between those who perceive deafness as a disability to be corrected and those who perceive deafness as membership in a minority linguistic culture, to be treasured and nurtured.[9] For many deaf people who perceive themselves as nondisabled members of a linguistic culture, it is natural to them to hope that their children share that culture by being deaf as well. Cochlear implants are a challenge to parents, who must make a difficult and largely irreversible choice for their children.

At present, the efficacy of cochlear implants when used with very young children who were born deaf appears modest at best. Most children in this category who have used them remain profoundly impaired in their hearing and speech. Meanwhile, the focus on joining the hearing world and the tremendous rehabilitative effort involved in using the implants to best advantage, have arguably deprived them of the opportunity to acquire sign language in an age-appropriate way. The enthusiasm of the scientific world for the use of cochlear implants even in prelingually deafened children betokens an attitude that any hearing is better than none and that the time and energy put into achieving even a tiny bit of speech is worth any sacrifice, even if that time is taken away from acquiring Sign. Thus, the current situation makes it easy to support decisions by parents not to choose implants for their deaf children. However, there is reason to expect that the technology will improve. If, in the future, the technology is perfected so that children born deaf will be able to hear and speak in normal fashion, what can we say about parents, deaf themselves, who decline to choose implants for their children?

The National Association for the Deaf (NAD) has condemned the decision of Food and Drug Administration (FDA) as "ethically unsound."[10] Other deaf activists have termed cochlear implant technology "sinister" and "genocidal."[11] Because 90 percent of deaf children are born to hearing parents, it is obvious that if most of these children can be "fixed" by the use of implants, the number of deaf people in America will shrink drastically, posing a serious threat to the continuance of "Deaf culture."[12] (In England, the sign used for cochlear implants is the same as the sign for the words "to kill.")[13] This makes some deaf parents even more determined not to rob their deaf children of their "birthright" of silence.[14] In fact, some people have made the argument that hearing parents of deaf children cannot make good decisions for their children's futures, at least where deafness and related issues are concerned. Think of the analogy of a white couple adopting an African-American baby at birth. The National Association of Black Social Workers has opposed transracial adoption because it deprives black children of their heritage.[15] Others have argued that white parents, however hard they try, cannot possibly understand what it means to be black, and thus cannot do a good job of raising black children. Black adults may well feel a connection to black children they see around them, even when they are strangers. In the same way, many deaf adults feel a connection and identity with deaf children, and feel that they have a stake in what happens to them.

> Deaf activists argue that in the case of cochlear implants, hearing parents have an inherent conflict of interest with their deaf child's best interest. Deaf activists contend that similar to the Jehovah's Witnesses who value their religious beliefs often to the extent of compromising their own children's health and welfare, hearing parents value their hearing to the extent of compromising their own children's health and welfare as well. .... Deaf activists conclude that because of the conflict of interest between hearing parents and deaf children, the court's presumptions that parents usually are in the best position to assess their child's needs and consistently act in their child's best interests should not apply in the case of cochlear implants.[16]

It is initially quite difficult for the average hearing person, who has not had much contact with deaf people, to think in terms of deaf culture and even to question the notion that any achievement of speech and hearing, no matter how imperfect, is worth any price. I remember seeing a television special on cochlear implants a few years ago. A little boy, about two years old, was profoundly deaf from birth. His parents were not deaf. In what the program presented as a "miracle of modern science," he had been fitted with a rather clunky device that allowed him to begin the laborious process of learning to hear. In this segment, his parents stood behind a closed door. The boy was supposed to listen for his mother's call, and open the door when he heard it. After a number of tries, he responded successfully by opening the door and tumbled, laughing, into his parents' arms; they lifted him with tears of gratitude in their eyes. The metaphor was unmistakable: a door had opened, a connection had been made. I had tears in my eyes myself. Not for a moment did it occur to me to ask why the parents were not spending some of their energies teaching themselves and the boy sign language. This door seemed to open only one way.

Deaf pride advocates point out that, as deaf people, they lack the ability to hear, but they also have many positive gains: a cohesive community, a rich cultural heritage built around the various residential schools,[17] a growing body of drama, poetry, and other artistic traditions, and, of course, what makes this all possible: ASL.[18] As the neurologist and popular author Oliver Sacks says, "Sign is the equal of speech, lending itself equally to the rigorous and the poetic—to philosophical analysis or to making love—indeed, with an ease that is sometimes greater than that of speech."[19]

It is important to note that deaf parents who would prefer to have deaf children are not only expressing an interest in having children who share the parents' mode of communication. They are saying that even if they could change themselves into hearing people (with hearing children), they would not. Roslyn Rosen, the president of the NAD, is deaf, the daughter of deaf parents, and the mother of deaf children. "I'm happy with who I am," she says, "and I don't want to be 'fixed.' Would an Italian-American rather be a WASP? In our society everyone agrees that whites have an easier time than blacks. But do you think a black person would undergo operations to become white?"[20] One of the ways in which deaf people differ from other physically disabled groups is that people who are blind or in wheelchairs do not hesitate to say that they would prefer to see or to walk, but people identified with the deaf culture movement generally say they would not make that choice.[21]

In 2002, an article in the *Washington Post* focused imagination on this issue, at home and abroad. The article featured an interview with a lesbian couple, Sharon Duchesneau and Candace McCullough, both of whom deaf, both graduates of Gallaudet, and who deliberately chose a sperm donor with five generations of deaf people in his family, in order to heighten the likelihood that their own children would be deaf. At the time of the interview, the couple had a (deaf) daughter, Jehanne, and were celebrating the birth of their (deaf) son, Gavin.[22] Deaf Studies scholar H-Dirksen L. Bauman asks, "Why did the reproductive choice of a single couple ignite such fury? Perhaps because it is an assault on standards of normalcy, turning them on their head, fashioning some new mutant strain of normalcy. And, the problem with normalcy is that it is not used to such competition."[23] (Interestingly, one of the couple's fiercest critics was British novelist Jeannette Winterson, who has written movingly about her childhood in a claustrophobic religious sect, and also about her lesbian orientation. Winterson likened the deaf couple to members of a psychotic religious sect who indoctrinate their children. "It is a simple fact," wrote Winterson, "that it is better to have five senses than four." To which Bauman replied, how would Winterson respond to the claim that it is "a simple fact" that it is better to be heterosexual than homosexual?[24] In fact, Ken Connor, president of a "pro-family" organization in Australia, wrote that the couple was "incredibly selfish" to heap on their children the disadvantages of deafness on top of "all the disadvantages that come as a result of being raised in a homosexual household."[25] Clearly, one person's normal variation is another person's disadvantage.)

Not all deaf people adhere to the notion of deaf culture, and some find the analogy to racial and ethnic groups "nonsensical."[26] Tucker says:

> Most of us would love to be able to pick up the telephone and make a personal or business call when and how we feel like it without having to scramble to find an interpreter and without having to make the call with

a third person privy to every word. We'd like to be able to go to a movie or a play regardless of whether captioning or interpreters are available. We'd like to be able to participate in group conversations, to hear the conversation at the dinner table. We'd like to be able to hear music; to hear our children and grandchildren laugh and cry; to listen to the radio when we are driving; to have a car phone; to be able to use the drive-up window at McDonald's; to hear the announcements at the airport; to be able to talk to the person in front of or behind us on a hiking trail; to be able to go to a professional meeting on the spur of the moment; to be able to get any job we want without having to consider how our deafness will interfere with the job duties. We'd particularly like to hear our own voices and to be able to control the tone and pitch and loudness of our voices. The list is endless. Why would any human being want to deny such pleasures to herself and her children?[27]

Tucker quotes another deaf person as saying:

[W]hat the hell is deaf pride? Proud not to hear your child's voice, pianos, the birds in the trees? That's not pride, it's bull-headedness and selfishness.[28]

Countering the deaf culture position, there is also evidence that deafness is a very serious disability. Deaf people have incomes well below the national average. In Australia, for example, a 2007 review of the literature found that compared to the rest of the community, deaf adults have had and continue to have higher unemployment rates, are underemployed in terms of the range of occupations, and typically earn less than the general population in similar occupations.[29] The state of education for the deaf is unacceptable by anyone's standards, in large part due to a continuing politicization of the debate between oral and ASL-based education; the typical deaf student graduates from high school are unable to read a newspaper.[30] Even among the brightest and most able deaf students, one reads heartbreaking accounts of the difficulties involved in tasks as simple as trying to sell an ad for the student yearbook.[31] However, one could also point to the lower incomes and inadequate state of education among some racial and ethnic minorities in our country, a situation we do not (or at least ought not) try to ameliorate by eradicating minorities.

Deaf advocates often cite the work of Nora Ellen Groce, whose oral history of Martha's Vineyard, *Everyone Here Spoke Sign Language*, tells a fascinating story.[32] For over two hundred years, ending in the middle of the twentieth century, the Vineyard experienced a degree of hereditary deafness exponentially higher than that of the mainland. The island was settled by a small number of people, mostly from an area in England with a history of hereditary deafness. Immigration to the Vineyard virtually ceased by 1710, and contact with outsiders was infrequent. The relatively isolated living conditions on the island fostered intermarriage and kept the rate of hereditary deafness high. On the island as a whole, the proportion of deaf people was 1 in 155, but in some towns, such as Chilmark, the number of deaf people in the mid-nineteenth century was 1 in 25. The result was a community in which deaf people had an economic prosperity on par with their neighbors and communicated easily with the rest of the island population, for "everyone here spoke sign language."[33] People who married into the community, even if no one in their family was deaf, learned sign language in order to fit in. One man who came from Gay Head, a town on the island populated almost exclusively by Native Americans and somewhat cutoff from the other towns, spoke of his discomfort at being unable to use sign language on his occasional forays to the general store in Chilmark: "You know, you would go down to Ernest Mayhew's store down there. I used to feel chagrined because I couldn't speak the sign language. ...I felt so dumb! They'd say things and make signs and look pleasant and God, I—it kind of embarrassed me because I couldn't understand."[34]

Sign was so much a part of the culture for the general population of the island that hearing islanders often exploited its unique properties even in the absence of deaf people. Old-timers told Groce stories of spouses communicating through sign language when they were outdoors and did not want to raise their voices against the wind. Or men might turn away and finish a "dirty" joke in sign when a woman walked into the general store. At church, deaf parishioners gave their testimony in sign.[35]

Groce concludes that "the concept of a handicap is an arbitrary social category."[36] Sociologist John B. Christiansen agrees, pointing out that we may now be at a peak in the level of disadvantage being deaf confers on one in our society. In the nineteenth and early twentieth centuries, telephones did not exist, and everyone enjoyed silent movies. Christiansen expects that, very soon, technology will allow deaf and hearing people to communicate over the telephone without the use of telecommunications device for the deaf (TDDs)[37] (just look at how e-mail is supplanting the telephone). As one deaf activist said, in a comment that could have been directly related to the Vineyard experience, "When Gorbachev visited the U.S., he used an interpreter to talk to the President. Was Gorbachev disabled?"[38] Looking at Tucker's list of what she misses out on because she is deaf, half of the situations could be easily ameliorated with presently available technology (e.g., electronic message boards as well as public address systems in airports, buttons to punch at the drive-up fast-food window).

Some disability scholars see a complete split between the social and the medical model of disability. The social model, taken to its extreme, discounts the biological limits of an impairment such as deafness, and attributes all limitations to societal indifference or even oppression.

The idea of the social model, which "turns the traditional definition of disability on its head," is seen by its advocates as the necessary ground for the disability rights movement.[39] "In our view, it is society which disables physically impaired people. Disability is something imposed on top of our impairments, by the way we are unnecessarily isolated and excluded from full participation in society."[40] The medical model, strenuously opposed by disability rights activists, focuses exclusively on the mechanics of impairment, gives control primarily to the doctors and scientists who seek to "cure" the impairment, and ignores the role played by society. Put crudely, one might ask: Is the problem the wheelchair—and is the response to cure the wheelchair user and get her out of the chair? Or is the problem the lack of elevators and curb cuts that would enable wheelchair users to access the same space as those who don't use chairs—and is the response therefore societal and legislative? Tom Shakespeare, a disabilities writer and activist who argues for a middle ground, sees disability as "a complex interaction between individual and structural factors."[41] One of Shakespeare's criticisms of the social model is that it ignores limitations that cannot be erased by even the most "barrier-free utopia." Nature, after all, cannot be blamed on social arrangements. "Wheelchair users are disabled by sandy beaches and rocky mountains. People with visual impairments may be unable to see a sunset, and people with hearing impairments will miss out on the sounds of birds, wind and waves."[42] Some Deaf culture proponents and Deaf Pride activists sidestep this problem by simply downplaying the importance of what they cannot hear, and playing up the importance of the strong bond and almost instant intimacy that exist within the deaf culture. "Communication and the pursuit of intimacy are central to being human. If you genuinely believe that your children will have at least as rich an emotional life if they cannot hear, and that you will be better able to communicate with them, why not make this choice?"[43]

Many of the problems that deaf people experience are the result of being born, without advance warning, to hearing parents. When there is no reason to anticipate the birth of a deaf child, it is often months or years before the child is correctly diagnosed. Meanwhile, he grows up in a world devoid of language, unable even to communicate with his parents. When the diagnosis is made, parents must first deal with the emotional shock and then sort through the plethora of conflicting advice on how best to raise and educate their child. Most probably they have never met anyone who is deaf. If they choose the route recommended by most deaf activists and raise their child with sign language, it will take parents years to learn ASL. Meanwhile, their child has missed out on the crucial development of language at the developmentally appropriate time, a lack associated with poor reading skills and other problems later on. Recent advances in testing most or all newborns' hearing soon after birth should mitigate this aspect of the problem.[44]

Further, even the most accepting of hearing parents often feel locked in conflict with the deaf community over who knows what is best for their child.[45] If deafness is truly a culture rather than a disability, then raising a deaf child is somewhat like white parents trying to raise a black child in contemporary America (with a background chorus of black activists trying to tell them that they cannot possibly make a good job of it). Residential schools, for example, which can be part of the family culture for a deaf couple, can be seen by hearing parents as Dickensian nightmares or, worse, as a "cultlike" experience in which their children will be lost to them forever.[46]

By contrast, deaf children born to deaf parents—"Deaf of Deaf," as they say—learn language (Sign) at the same age as hearing children. They are welcomed into their families and inculcated into deaf culture in the same way as any other children are welcomed into their own culture. By all accounts and perhaps for these reasons, the Deaf of

Deaf are the acknowledged leaders of the Deaf Pride movement and the academic *crème de la crème*, "the eloquent ones, the skilled communicators of the Deaf community."[47] At Gallaudet, all four leaders of the Deaf President Now movement were Deaf of Deaf.[48] In evaluating the parental choice deliberately to ensure having deaf children, one must remember that the statistics and descriptions of deaf life in America are largely reflective of the experience of deaf children born to hearing parents, who make up over 90 percent of deaf people today.[49]

Deaf parents who are taken aback to find themselves with a hearing baby may exhibit many of the same discomforts as hearing parents of deaf babies, in reverse. The following account is from an interview with a deaf woman, describing the birth of her daughter:

> When Barbara was born, it wasn't until about three days later that I had this funny feeling about her. I started wondering if she was deaf or hearing. ... My first child. I kept wondering to myself, Is she deaf or hearing? I was holding her in my arms near the metal food tray. I picked up a spoon and dropped it on the tray. I couldn't believe it! I was really upset. I did it a second time because I just couldn't believe it. I dropped the spoon again and it was the same thing. I even did it a third time. I thought, Oh, my God, she's hearing! What am I going to do? I have a hearing daughter! My husband came in and I said My God, our daughter's hearing! He was just as surprised but he told me it was fine, it was going to be okay. I'm the third generation deaf. There was no question but that we would have deaf children. Then I find out that my daughter was born hearing! What on earth am I going to do with her? I don't even know how to talk to her. ["So you never thought that you might have a hearing child?"] No, never! It never occurred to me that my child would be hearing. I was really surprised. I was scared. I wanted to be close to my children. I've always been very

close to my family, and I wanted the same for me and my children. The Hearing world and the Deaf world are such separate worlds. I worried that we would never connect, or that we would drift apart.[50]

One obvious response to the concerns of deaf parents about raising hearing children is that being hearing does not preclude learning sign language and participating fully in family life, and deaf culture. A hearing child born of deaf parents could, theoretically, "have it all." However, as Judith Rich Harris points out (and as the film and fiction portraying the immigrant experience poignantly recounts), children tend to gravitate to the mainstream culture in which they are raised, even if their family has a different language and customs. "When in Rome, do as the Romans do. For children it's more than that: when in Rome, they become Romans. Even if their parents happen to be British or Chinese or Mesquakie. When the culture outside the home differs from the culture inside it, the outside culture wins."[51] Perhaps there is a parallel here with the Amish I discussed in Chapter 1. Those Amish feared that, once their children were given the tools and exposure to the dominant culture, they would either choose not to return to the Amish way of life, or even be psychologically unable to accept and flourish within the narrow limits of Amish culture. Like Deaf activists today, the Amish feared not only the tension within individual families, but the death of their entire religion. At the same time, one has to question the strength and richness of a culture that can only hang on to its adherents by denying them the tools to leave.

I suspect that one reason Deaf parents can be so disturbed at the thought of raising hearing children is that their own experience as deaf kids was often marked by extreme social isolation, even within their nuclear families. "The Deaf identity is in large part a product of a shared sense of isolation from the hearing world. Exclusion is central to the experience."[52] Surely, any prospective parent would fear the possibility that such isolation could mark their own family, and come between them and their child. So perhaps it is no surprise that deaf adults are not always eager to use genetic techniques to avoid the "risk" of deaf babies, and that a significant number of deaf adults actively prefer to have deaf children. "If their children are not likely to be born deaf, Deaf parents may choose not to have children, or to abort children in gestation, just as hearing or deaf people who determine through genetic research that their children are likely to be born deaf may choose not to have children or to abort children in gestation."[53] As Arnos, Israel, and Cunningham, of the Genetics Service Center at Gallaudet University, have written, "It is often difficult for medical practitioners to realize that terms such as 'risk' of having a deaf child, and 'affected' or 'abnormal' are terms that can have a very negative impact for someone who views their deafness not as a pathology but as a cultural difference. ... Deaf couples may consider it a 'risk' to have a hearing child rather than a deaf child."[54] A 1998 study of delegates to Deaf Nation, an international conference in Great Britain, garnered some interesting data. The attitude toward genetics and genetic counseling was "predominantly negative." Genetics was seen as a "threat," both to individual persons and couples approaching counselors, and to the deaf community at large, as it threatened to reduce their numbers. The majority of delegates thought genetic testing would do "more harm than good." When asked their preference for deaf or hearing children, 15 percent preferred deaf children, and 74 percent were neutral.[55] Although this was a small study, the results are in line with a 1996 study in which 19 percent of a sample of 74 deaf and hard-of-hearing college students expressed a preference for deaf children.[56]

These figures are disputed. In any case, having a preference is quite different from using deliberative procreation to ensure having a deaf child. Barbara Biesecker, a genetic counselor at National

Institutes of Health (NIH), warns that, "It is offensive to keep harping on this scenario. While many deaf parents may harbor a preference for having deaf children, the data suggest that the majority would never consider doing it."[57] It is probably true that faced with the decision to have children the old-fashioned way and leave the child's hearing status up to chance, versus the expense and difficulties of using reproductive technologies, most deaf parents would leave it to chance, no matter what their preferences are. However, as in the general population, deaf people are increasingly making use of assisted reproductive technologies (ART) for other reasons. Sharon and Candace are among an increasing number of lesbian and gay couples using ART to have babies. Other deaf people, like people everywhere in the West, are marrying and having children later, and making use of assisted reproduction to overcome infertility. Perhaps other couples have lethal genes in their family and use ART to avoid a tragedy. In all these cases, with the decision already made to use ART, it becomes much easier to decide to make sure, or at least to increase the chances, that the baby is deaf. Had Candace and Sharon each been part of a heterosexual couple that faced no fertility problems, the thought of ensuring a deaf child might not have even occurred to them; but since they had to make use of a sperm donor in any case, why not a deaf one? If a couple is using PGD to avoid Tay-Sachs disease, why not also check for genetically based deafness? The majority of IVF-PGD clinic directors believe that future technology will permit whole genome embryo screening as a routine part of IVF, so all of the embryos' genetic characteristics will be laid out for prospective parents. Thus, as ART becomes more common across all groups of people, the gap between those deaf couples who might "harbor a preference," and those who might act on that preference, is likely to narrow. Already, 3 percent of IVF-PGD clinics report having provided PGD to couples "who seek to use PGD to select an embryo for the presence of a disability."[58]

The Arnos paper presents a good example of the issue we are looking at in this chapter. "Genetic counseling," the authors remind us, "is a communication process where information is provided in a nondirective way. ... [G]enetic counseling is not advice giving."[59] They agree with other geneticists who have written that "genetic counseling should promote individual needs rather than societal goals."[60] They acknowledge that "[g]enetic counseling for a deaf individual or couple, who may prefer to have deaf children, may challenge the genetic counselor to examine their own approach to nondirective counseling."[61] In other words, how should the genetic counselor respond when the deaf couple asks her assistance in trying to ensure that they have only deaf children?

Does Creating Deaf Children Violate the Child's Right to an Open Future?

If deafness is a culture rather than a disability, it is an exceedingly narrow one. One factor that does not seem clear is the extent to which children raised with Sign as their first language, a *sine qua non* of the deaf culture perspective, will ever be comfortable with the written word. Sign itself has no written analogue and has a grammatical structure completely different from that of English. At present the conflicted and politicized state of education for the deaf, along with the many hours spent (some would say wasted) on learning oral skills, makes it impossible to know what is to blame for the dismal reading and writing skills of the average deaf person.[62] Some deaf children raised with Sign from birth do become skilled readers, but there is reason to question whether a deaf child has access to the wealth of literature, drama, and poetry that liberals would like to consider every child's birthright.

Although deaf activists correctly show that many occupations are open to the deaf with only minor technological adjustments, the range of occupations will always be inherently limited. It is unlikely that the world will become like Martha's Vineyard, where everyone knew how to sign. This narrow choice of vocation is not only a harm in its own sake, but also is likely to continue to lead to lower standards of living. Certainly, one reason why the Vineyard deaf had the same level of prosperity as their hearing neighbors was that farming and fishing were just about the only occupations available to any residents back then, whether hearing or deaf.

Thus, in my opinion, less rides on where you come out on the disability-versus-culture debate than first appears. If deafness is a disability that substantially narrows a child's career, marriage, and cultural options, then deliberately creating a deaf child counts as a moral harm, because it so dramatically curtails the child's right to an open future. If deafness is a culture, as deaf activists assert, then deliberately creating a deaf child who will have only limited options to move outside of that culture also counts as a moral harm. Even William Galston, who argues that liberalism is about the protection of diversity rather than of individual autonomy, begins with the presumption that society must "defend ... the liberty not to be coerced into, or trapped within, ways of life. Accordingly, the state must safe-guard the ability of individuals to shift allegiances and cross boundaries."[63] A decision made before a child is born that confines him forever to a narrow group of people and a limited choice of careers so violates the child's right to an open future that no genetic counselor should acquiesce to it. The very value of autonomy that grounds the ethics of genetic counseling should preclude assisting parents in such a decision.

What are the implications of this conclusion for parents who must decide on cochlear implants for their nonhearing children? Assuming that the implants become more effective in the near future, I would argue that parents have an obligation to have their children implanted. Amy Elizabeth Brusky puts it in terms too clear to improve upon:

> [T]he issue is one of choice and options. Without a cochlear implant, a deaf child has no choice. The child is resigned to deafness. With an implant, however, the hearing world becomes another option in addition to the deaf community.

Deaf activists argue that an implant will eliminate a child's choice to develop a cultural identity linked to the use of American Sign Language. However, deaf persons who gain the ability to hear do not lose their sense of who they are, unless they unreasonably have chosen to define themselves solely in terms of their deafness. The development of a child's sense of self depends upon so many other diverse factors, including moral and religious upbringing, ethnicity, nationality and more. Moreover, an implanted child is not precluded from eventually choosing not to wear the implant's external parts and deciding to follow the deaf cultural lifestyle. However, having the implant first will at least give a child a choice and provide him or her with the advantages of biculturalism and the opportunity to function in both worlds.[64]*

---

* I am discussing here only the case of nonhearing parents, whether Deaf or deaf. It is possible that hearing parents might seriously consider the possibility of not fitting their deaf child with implants, even if those implants were effective in allowing the child to speak and hear with near-normal facility. But this is a rare case, surely, and it is hard to fathom their motivation.

And what about Celia and others like her, who would like to ensure that their children have achondroplasia? This issue, it seems to me, is a much more difficult judgment call (perhaps only because less has been studied and written about the world of "little people" and the extent to which their cultural, social, and career choices are constrained by their condition). True, a child born achondroplasic because of his parents' manipulations cannot reverse their decision and choose to become of average stature, but it does not seem that momentous pieces of his adult life will be foreclosed by that decision. Thus, I am less clear that genetic counselors should refuse to help Celia and her husband in their quest to ensure a child who is like them.

At this point my argument may appear to be open to a very serious criticism. After all, many parents have children in situations in which their lives will be quite narrow and difficult, or at least more difficult than the norm. Am I saying that poor, illiterate people in developing nations should not have children, because their children are likely to be poor and illiterate as well, and thus have extremely constrained lives? Is having an African-American baby a moral wrong, because African Americans have a more difficult time in our country than white people? What about would-be parents in Appalachia or our inner cities, where the prevailing cultures can also be very difficult to exit?

The norm I want to propose is something like "Parents ought not *deliberately* to substantively constrain the ability of their children to make a wide variety of life choices when they become adults." By including the criterion of voluntariness, I limit my criticism to parents who have choices about the world they offer their children. Thus, I am not criticizing deaf couples who have no choice but to have deaf children, and who decide nonetheless to become parents. Nor am I criticizing people who have children under less than optimal conditions because of societal injustice, for example, members of oppressed minority groups. In that case, the appropriate criticism is directed at the oppressors, and one of the worst evils of oppressive societies is precisely the way in which they constrain the future of the minority children who are marginalized.

Should we Regulate Reproductive Genetics?

When Sharon Dechesneau and Candace McCullough made public their decision to use a deaf sperm donor in the hope of having deaf children, many people were outraged. William Saletan of *Slate* magazine coined the term "deformer babies" to describe what the women had done. "Old fear: designer babies. New fear: deformer babies."[65] Many Americans experience deep unease, when faced with some of the new possibilities inherent in reproductive technology. As we shall see in Chapter 5, sex selection for nonmedical reasons is frequently condemned (but frequently practiced). The use of PGD to ensure that a new baby will indeed be a "savior sibling" who can donate precious bone marrow to a dying sibling, is also controversial. Although there is certainly no dearth of books, articles, TV presentations and the like, the United States lacks a central public forum in which to hash these issues out.

In the United States, reproductive technology, prenatal genetic diagnosis, and PGD are all virtually unregulated. Federal regulatory agencies (such as the FDA) touch only tangentially on the core issue of when PGD is appropriate. There are no state laws directly addressing PGD, although there are some laws that relate to assisted reproductive technology. But even these laws are concerned primarily with issues of insurance, informed consent, and defining parentage.[66] This is in contrast to many other countries. PGD is outlawed in Switzerland, Germany and Australia, for example, and heavily regulated in the United Kingdom[67] In the United Kingdom, the Human Fertilisation and Embryology Authority (HFEA) has sole authority to regulate how PGD is used in all of the country's licensed clinics. The United Kingdom also regulates medical decisions such as how many embryos created through IVF can be put into the uterus at one time. Some countries forbid offering IVF to unmarried women, to postmenopausal women, and so on.

In the United States, therefore, issues such as choosing embryos for a disability, or for the desired gender, are discussed through the media, and often in a report by one or another presidential bioethics commissions and government advisory committees, none of them influential or efficacious, and none with a high public profile.[68] In contrast, a recent survey showed that 59 percent of the British public had heard of the HFEA, with 31 percent saying that they knew something of its work.[69] This is not surprising, as HFEA goes to great lengths to hold public hearings and information sessions. Perhaps more important, since the HFEA actually regulates, its deliberations hold serious implications for the daily lives of many in the United Kingdom.

It is instructive to contrast the flap over the Duchesneau-McCullough baby in the United States with the contentious passage of the British HFEA in 2009. The HFEA was set up in 1991 as part of the Human Fertilisation and Embryology Act of 1990. Its principal tasks are to license and monitor clinics that carry out IVF, artificial insemination, and human embryo research (including PGD). Other nongovernmental organizations in Britain, such as the Progress Educational Trust and the Wellcome Trust, do a great deal of educational programming in schools and in the community, around issues involving the HFEA, genetics, and reproduction.

Clause 14 of the 2009 Act amending the HFEA (which has since become law) had important implications for deaf people. The Clause prohibits a person with "a serious genetic condition" from donating sperm for IVF if a donor without such a condition exists. It also requires that an embryo with the genes for "a serious condition" must not be implanted if there is an available embryo without the genes for a serious known genetic condition. Explanatory notes accompanying the Bill specifically used the example of deafness as a "serious condition."[70] So, if sperm donation is to be accomplished through IVF (not necessarily the case) a deaf couple such as Sharon and Candace could not avail themselves of a deaf sperm donor. And a deaf couple could not use IVF and PGD to ensure the birth of a deaf child. To be clear, a deaf couple, even a couple that needs IVF, is under no compulsion to genetically test their embryos. But once they do test, they may not choose a deaf embryo if a nonimpaired embryo is available.

The British couple who in some ways captured the public imagination the way Duchesneau and McCullough did in the States, is a heterosexual married pair, Tomato Lichy and Paula Garfield, who are both deaf and who have a three-year-old deaf daughter. Because Paula is in her 40s, they believe they may need IVF to have another child, and might also wish to use PGD to test for what they consider to be serious genetic diseases. They have publicly expressed their interest in also using PGD to choose a deaf embryo. The British Deaf Association (BDA) and the Royal National Institute for Deaf and Hard of Hearing People, while not coming out in favor of choosing deaf embryos, nonetheless opposed the Bill because it denied to deaf people the same freedom of choice that hearing people have. The Chair of the BDA said, "If choice of embryos for implantation is to be given to citizens in general, and if hearing and other people are allowed to choose embryos that will be 'like them,' sharing the same characteristics, language and culture, then we believe that deaf people should have the same right."[71] Because everyone agreed that the number of deaf couples who might actually use IVF and PGD to choose a deaf baby was tiny, a number of commentators thought that the HFEA should leave well enough alone. Nonetheless, the Bill did eventually pass.

It may seem strange to American ears that the state could tell you which kind of babies you can produce through genetic and reproductive technologies. However, some U.S. policy scholars are advocating a less laissez-faire approach in this country as well. Some believe that "decisions about technologies so profound that they could shape future generations should not be left entirely to the discretion of individual parents and providers. They raise concerns about the inappropriate use of reproductive genetic tests and believe that broader societal consensus and input are needed."[72] Although professional societies of physicians and geneticists have published guidelines for their members, such guidelines are usually voluntary, without sanctions. The American Society for Reproductive Medicine (ASRM), for example, published an opinion of its ethics committee, advising against the use of PGD for sex selection, in the absence of a medical reason. However, there are ASRM members who offer and advertise sex selection services for "social" reasons.[73] In any case, even the best guidelines reflect only an internal discussion within the profession, not a robust public debate.

The Genetics & Public Policy Center issued a report attempting to show all the pros and cons of different policy options, from the (unregulated) status quo, to regulation by private parties (e.g., third party payers) and the federal government. The Center listed a number of arguments in favor of federal or state regulation on the HFEA model. Government restrictions would create a clear line about what is permissible, "providing legally enforceable rules based on shared societal values." The process of creating legal rules would "stimulate a productive public discussion about how to effectively oversee genetic testing and what limits are appropriate." Arguments against government regulation included the privacy argument, reminiscent of *Roe v. Wade*, that such rules would be a "significant intrusion" into decisions best left to patients and medical personnel. Enforcement of the rules would also involve significant intrusion into people's reproductive behavior, such as attempting to find out after the fact why testing, or subsequent abortion, was performed, or why a specific embryo was chosen. Further, one could argue that there is not enough societal consensus to ground a productive public debate.[74]

A problem with legal constrictions is that it puts a heavy penalty on couples who, for reasons of infertility, genetic trait, or sexual orientation, are forced to make use of reproductive technology, and thus open up their reproductive choices to public scrutiny and control. This is the "gatekeeper" problem. Another contentious aspect of the new HFEA Act was whether it should continue to require IVF clinics to take into account the best interests of the future child, when deciding whether or not to take on a person or couple as clients. It seems hard to argue *against* considering the best interests of the child (and I would not make that argument) but opponents of the clause pointed out that it was often used to discriminate against people (lesbian couples, racially mixed couples, etc.) of whom the clinic personnel disapproved.

The gatekeeper question is, if two people with terrible genetic histories—imagine a couple of whom both members have the gene for Huntington Disease (HD)—can still do as they please reproductively, as long as they can conceive naturally, why should a clinic doctor or the state be able to tell that couple that they can't conceive just because they need some technical assistance? Is that not unfair? Imagine a couple where both the man and the woman have achondroplasia. If they do not use IVF and PGD, they face a 25 percent chance of having a terrible tragedy: a child with two copies of the gene, who will surely die. But if they live in the United Kingdom and want to avail themselves of IVF and PGD to avoid that tragedy, they will also be required to choose an embryo of normal stature (if one exists in the pool of embryos they create) over an embryo who will grow up to be a dwarf. Given that the same couple could simply reproduce naturally with no legal coercion, is it fair of the state to exploit its gatekeeper status to deny them this reproductive option?

The gatekeeper problem is not, of course, confined to genetics. Two people who are TB-infected drug addicts, with no jobs, may conceive and give birth any time they want, with no interference. Does that mean that the same couple, if they could come up with the money (or live in a country where reproductive services are publicly provided), must be given technical assistance to achieve that goal? As you know from previous chapters, I do believe that gatekeepers such as geneticists have a moral obligation to take account of the child's welfare, including its right to an open future. I do not believe that that obligation is outweighed by the argument that justice requires that people be offered technical assistance to accomplish bad outcomes, just because other couples could accomplish those same outcomes naturally.

An HFEA-like regulatory agency in the United States would have some obvious advantages. The rules could, for example, make it clear that clinics cannot turn away single women, or mixed-race families. (Of course, other antidiscrimination laws may already do that job.) But given our long history of abortion "debate," which can barely be dignified by the term, I doubt that a debate over the proper use of PGD would accomplish very much, especially as there is a strong segment of American society that opposes all IVF and PGD because of the embryo wastage involved. Any public discussion over regulating reproductive genetics would inevitably get pulled into America's contentious abortion debate (a topic that generates much less heat in the United Kingdom).

Childhood Testing for Genetic Traits

4

The Reimers are a couple in their thirties who live in Montreal. They have a six-year-old boy, Josh, and a four-year-old girl, Sarah. Rob and Miriam are struggling to recover from a major tragedy. Their third child, a little boy named Daniel, recently died at the age of two, from Tay-Sachs disease. Rob and Miriam had had no idea that they might be carriers and were stunned by Daniel's diagnosis. Although Miriam had always been active in the Jewish community, Rob had grown up in a nonreligious, unaffiliated family, with a Jewish father and non-Jewish mother, and didn't really think of himself as Jewish. Thus the Reimers had not paid much attention to the various public service announcements about the prevalence of Tay-Sachs disease in the Jewish community and the advantages of genetic testing.

Rob and Miriam both come from large families and had always planned on having at least four children. Now, as they come to terms with their grief over Daniel's death and recover from the exhaustion

*occasioned by his long illness, they are also grappling with some chal-
lenging decisions. Should they thank their lucky stars that Josh and
Sarah are healthy, and give up their hopes for a larger family? Should
they enlarge their family by adoption instead? Should they conceive
again but test the fetus for Tay-Sachs and abort if it is affected?
Should they conceive through in vitro fertilization (IVF) and implant
only embryos free from the disease? Now that the Reimers understand
that carrier status can be determined by a simple blood test, they are
also wondering whether they should have Josh and Sarah tested as
well. Rob tends to think of Daniel's death as his "fault." Had Rob
been more aware of his Jewish heritage, and had he listened early on
to information about Tay-Sachs, he and Miriam would have gotten
tested and the tragedy would have been averted. Rob reasons that
there is no telling where Josh and Sarah may be living when they
marry and begin their families. Montreal has a free program for Tay-
Sachs carrier testing, and Rob wants to have the kids tested now, so
that the parents can inform them of their status when the right time
comes.*

THIS CHAPTER TAKES UP a slightly different type of problem than those in
the surrounding chapters. In Chapters 3, 5, and 6 we look at things
that parents can do to actually create children in a certain manner,
for example, making sure that their children have achondroplasia,
are girls rather than boys, or are cloned from existing human beings.
In this chapter we remain with our basic theme: how decisions that
parents make about genetics can expand or limit their children's
future possibilities. But we look not at what parents can do but at
what they can *know*. What kinds of genetic knowledge are available

to parents about their children, how is that knowledge obtained, and what are the ethical ramifications of the parental search for genetic information? In the first part of the chapter we will look at a problem that has been well discussed in the ethics literature: childhood testing for late-onset genetic disease. In the second part we will look at a less discussed and more subtle issue: parental knowledge of their children's carrier status for recessive genetic disease.

Childhood Testing for Late-Onset Genetic Disease

A number of serious genetic diseases do not show themselves until fairly late in life. A person with Huntington disease (HD), for example, does not usually begin to exhibit symptoms of the disease until the fourth or fifth decade. Huntington is a neurological disorder that causes uncontrollable jerking and writhing movements all over the body. (The older name for this disease is Huntington's chorea; chorea means "movement" and comes from the same root as choreography.) Worse even than these movements is the progressive cognitive degeneration, which can lead to emotional disturbance, severe depression, and hallucinations. Eventually the person becomes unable to move. Woody Guthrie is probably the most famous American to fall victim to HD. Some of us remember the touching scene in Arlo Guthrie's movie *Alice's Restaurant* in which Arlo and Pete Seeger are visiting Woody Guthrie in his hospital room and break into an impromptu hootenanny. Throughout the scene, Woody just lies there, unable to do anything more than blink his eyes.

HD is caused by a single gene, one that is transmitted in an autosomal dominant inheritance pattern. In other words, if you have even one copy of the gene, you will certainly be affected by HD (unless something else kills you first). If one of your parents has the gene, then you have a 50 percent chance of inheriting the gene and, as a result, the disease.[1] Occurring so late in life is a clever strategy of a gene like this. Unlike a fatal recessive gene such as the one for Tay-Sachs disease, which can survive "undercover" for generations, if a gene such as the one for HD affected its victims too early, they would fail to reproduce and the gene itself would soon be out of business. Instead, until recently, people with the HD gene were forced to make reproductive decisions without knowing their own fate and without knowing whether or not they were at risk of passing the gene on to their children. That changed in 1986, when a pre-symptomatic genetic test for HD became available.[2]

One would probably think that the availability of such a test would be greeted with unalloyed joy and that everyone who thought she was at risk (due to family history) would rush to be tested. The actual experience has been very different. Knowing one's HD status has numerous pros and cons (even when one finds out that one is free of the gene). The advantages are, first, that persons at risk can now make reproductive decisions knowing whether or not they have a 50 percent chance of passing the gene to their children. Second, those who find out that they do not have the gene for HD will presumably be more relaxed, not constantly worrying whether every passing hand tremor is the first sign of incipient HD. As one writer pointed out:

> [T]he symptoms [of HD] can begin at any time, from very early to very late. So the worry is essentially life-long. Every clumsy movement, every slight stumble, any momentary slurring of speech or fleeting unsteadiness of gait-trivial events most people would ignore-will, in the individual at risk for HD, arouse apprehensions: Is this it? Does the inexorable decline now begin?[3]

Finally, people who know that they carry the gene will be able to make decisions regarding their future, including provisions for long-term care.

However, in the years since testing has become available, a number of disadvantages have become obvious as well. Discovering that one definitely has HD can lead to depression, social stigma, and problems with insurance and employment.[4] Even knowing that one does not have the gene can lead to "survivor guilt" and serious psychological problems if any of one's siblings were not so lucky. Thus only 15 percent of adults at risk have availed themselves of the opportunity to be tested and to discover their status.[5]

This mixed reaction to the option of presymptomatic testing raises a difficult ethical question: How should health care providers respond to parents who wish to have their children tested for adult onset genetic disorders for which there is no possible medical intervention or surveillance strategy? (Of course, if testing now could facilitate some strategy of diet, medication, or surveillance that would prevent or ameliorate the disease, there would be no ethical question but that parents should have their children tested, as testing would clearly be in the child's best interest.) At present there is a consensus among genetics professionals in Europe and the United States that predictive genetic testing of children "should generally not be undertaken" if there are no useful medical interventions.[6] However, this is a consensus of ethicists and working groups focused on the issue, not of practicing physicians and geneticists, nor of parents. On the one hand, a survey of all guidelines and position papers on this topic showed unanimity in postponing testing until the child could consent as a competent adolescent or adult.[7] On the other hand, a 1993 survey in the United Kingdom showed that a majority of pediatricians and a substantial minority of geneticists would test children at the parents' request for late-onset genetic disorders or for unaffected carrier status.[8] Many people are of the opinion that just as other medical decisions about children are within the parents' control, so it is the parents' right to make this decision as well.

There are many reasons why parents may request presymptomatic genetic testing of children for adult-onset diseases, even in the absence of any useful medical intervention. Parents may hope for a reduction in their own uncertainty and anxiety, or hope to alleviate guilt they may feel about passing along an inheritable disease. They may use the information to make decisions about whether or not to have more children or how to space subsequent pregnancies. Parents may want to take genetic predictions into account as they allocate resources for higher education or consider other kinds of long-range planning. One genetics center had a man request testing of his grandchildren in order to decide how to write his will (the center turned him down).[9] Another reason to have a child tested, perhaps as a teenager, might be to avoid the psychological disruption of living an at-risk role that is later repudiated. Nancy Wexler, herself at risk for HD, reported on a pilot testing program with extensive counseling begun at the College of Physicians and Surgeons at Columbia University, and noted:

> It is almost as inconceivable for people to learn that they are not in harm's way. Identities have been built around being "at risk": commitments abandoned, lives led in the fast lane. Some people who learn that they are free of the long-dreaded gene are stunned and unprepared. Suddenly they are ordinary; vulnerable now to other diseases, responsible for their lives as never before. Friends and relatives who had sacrificed for them in the past may feel cheated and vengeful or disturbed to find themselves deprived of their role of tending to an invalid.[10]

There is, of course, a strong tradition in our law and culture of allowing parents great latitude in making medical decisions for their children. We make exceptions to that rule in the case of so-called mature minors, in research protocols (where children are barred from risky research even if their parents consent), or when parents' decisions put children at great risk of losing their lives or their health, as when Jehovah's Witnesses attempt to refuse necessary blood transfusions for their children. But outside of those exceptions, it is still the case that a parental decision is both necessary and sufficient for providing medical care for minor children. This tradition began with the premodern doctrine that the child was the father's property. Today it rests on three assumptions: that parents are the persons most able to make a decision about the well-being and best interests of their children; that safeguarding the health and well-being of their children is a legal and moral responsibility of parents; and that making decisions about children's education, medical care, and so on is part of the autonomy rights of parents as heads of their families. Thus, when a genetic test has been placed before the public, geneticists are up against a powerful presumption if they refuse parental requests.

Geneticists make a number of arguments against acceding to parental requests for predictive testing. They fear that a child with a genetic defect will be subjected to increased medical tests and treatment regimens with no proven benefit, may suffer a loss of self-esteem, may experience a loss of privacy if the diagnosis is disclosed outside the immediate family, may be stigmatized in school or in future employment, or may have difficulty obtaining insurance later in life.[11]

A report prepared by the boards of directors of the American Society of Human Genetics and the American College of Medical Genetics attempts to resolve this issue by relying on the basic tenet of all medical ethics: *primum non nocere*, or "first do no harm." It acknowledges, however, that where the benefits and harms "are primarily psychosocial rather than medical, such an assessment may be difficult."[12] Pediatrician and ethicist Eric Kodish has advocated "the rule of earliest onset," arguing that "genetic testing should be permitted at an age no earlier than the age of first possible onset of the [disease]," or at the earliest age at which an intervention is possible.[13] (When the disease is breast cancer, for example, the age of earliest onset would translate to the age at which it would make medical sense to begin mammograms.) Advocates of the parental right to make the decision rely on "the privacy of the family unit in our culture" and frame the issue as one of tension between "the beneficence model of patient care and the rights of parents to their own autonomy and to the protection of their family units."[14]

The concept of the child's right to an open future provides a new pathway toward resolving this problem. Although the majority of adults at risk for HD have decided not to be tested, 15 percent have chosen the other route. Thus, there is no accepted and common answer to the question of whether life is better lived with or without the knowledge of one's HD status. A recent study of a large group of people who have one parent with HD, but who have decided not to be tested, shows how uncertainty can be a successful strategy; these people maintain an intricate balance between living with risk and living with hope. "The central role that uncertainty plays in preserving hope for the future" further convinced the authors of this study of the wisdom of the guidelines against testing children for adult-onset disease such as HD.[15]

Genetic counselors go to great lengths to protect the right of adults to make the decision for themselves whether or not to be tested. If parents have the child tested, then they preclude the child's right and opportunity to make that decision for himself in adulthood. As we have seen, for those unfortunate enough to have a family history of a disease like HD, the decision whether or not to be tested is profound and complex. Sometimes siblings, or even identical twins, will come to different conclusions. Psychologically speaking, even the lucky 50 percent who discover that they do not have the gene are hardly home free. This is a decision each individual can make only for herself. Thus respect for the child's right to an open future supports the growing consensus in the United States against allowing parents to choose such testing for their children.

This conclusion does not preclude the possibility of genetic testing for a mature minor who requests the test on her own initiative and continues to request testing after appropriate counseling. This is analogous to allowing older teenagers to make their own medical decisions, on a case-by-case basis.[16] Young people in families affected by diseases such as HD or Fragile X are usually well aware of their risk, and at some point they may decide to trade their uncertainty for knowledge. With proper counseling there is no reason to deny mature adolescents this choice. One study of girls who knew that they were at risk for being carriers of Fragile X syndrome, concluded that information about genetic risk is more threatening than actual information about carrier status. Adolescent girls who discovered that they were carriers had real concerns about future parenthood, and girls who discovered that they were not carriers expressed relief, but both sets of girls were able to incorporate the knowledge into a positive self-image and get on with the task of becoming adults. Girls who did not know their carrier status reported great uncertainty, barriers to friendships, and emotional distress.[17]

At a certain point in their maturity, acceding to rational adolescent requests for genetic testing can be in young people's best interests, because respect for their autonomy can support self-esteem and psychological health.[18] To quote the policy statement of the American Academy of Pediatrics, "When the results of genetic testing will be used solely for future reproductive decisions or when parents request it and there are no benefits to the child, in most circumstances it should be deferred until the child can request such testing as an autonomous individual who is able to appreciate the emotional and social consequences, as well as the genetic facts, of the results."[19] Many older adolescents, while still legal minors, fit that description.

I do not agree with Kodish's rule of earliest onset when the disease is one that will appear in early childhood, such as Duchenne muscular dystrophy. Arguments against testing for these diseases, even without an effective intervention, are that premature knowledge may disrupt parent/child bonding, cast the child into a "sick role" prematurely, and in genetic diseases of variable penetrance, raise fears unnecessarily.[20] However, there are equally good arguments on the other side. Families may need to know whether they are likely to have a child with special medical needs when choosing where to live, or whether to prefer a job with solid medical benefits to the riskier life of an entrepreneur. Because the disease will strike before the child is an adult in any case, there are no concerns here about protecting the autonomy of the child to choose to be tested as an adult.

A related issue deals with confidentiality. Although I will take up this topic more fully in the coming pages, with respect to parental discovery of children's carrier status for recessive genes, it is worth saying a word about it now. Genetic counselors will protect without exception the right of individuals not to share their genetic information with others, even in situations where not sharing the information puts others at risk or limits their options. We normally do not think of medical confidentiality as an issue between parents and children, outside of the reproductive area, because of the overriding assumption that parents need to know about their children's medical conditions in order to promote their health and well-being. Thus, it would be ludicrous for a doctor to refuse to share with a parent the results of a child's test for tuberculosis or asthma. But in the case of HD, there is nothing the parent can do to prevent the disease from occurring, and arguably little the parent can do to prepare the child, younger than eighteen, for a disease that probably will not strike until middle age. Thus, it appears that the right of privacy that the child will have when she becomes an adult, to decide what medical and genetic information she will choose to share with her family, should be respected now and not sabotaged by allowing her parents to have her tested.

Discovery of Children's Carrier Status for Recessive Genetic Diseases

In the previous pages I focused on testing children for genetic diseases that will not affect them physically until adulthood. HD is a good paradigm for thinking about this problem, because of its autosomal dominant pattern and its "complete penetrance": if you have the gene for HD, the disease will get you in the end. Now we will turn our attention to diseases on the opposite end of the genetic spectrum: recessive genetic disorders that, unless you have inherited genes for the disease from both of your parents, will never physically affect you. Just as HD has been a paradigm for the first type of genetic disorder, Tay-Sachs has often functioned as a model of the second type.

Because Tay-Sachs is a recessive disease, a person can be affected only if both the parents are carriers of the gene. Even where both parents are carriers, the chances of getting the "bad" gene from both of your parents is only one out of four. By the same token, there is a one in four chance that you inherited two "good" genes from your parents, and are neither affected nor a carrier. The most likely outcome—one out of two—is that you inherited one problem gene from one parent and one good gene from the other and that you are a carrier, just like your parents. You will never have any health problems due to your carrier status, but if you marry another carrier of Tay-Sachs disease, your children will face the same statistical odds for having the disease or being carriers.

In the general population, one in three hundred people are carriers, but the incidence of Tay-Sachs is much higher in certain ethnic groups. French Canadians have a high rate of Tay-Sachs disease. Among Ashkenazi (European) Jews, one in thirty is a carrier. The chance of two Ashkenazi Jews having a double-carrier marriage is one in nine hundred. Because this is a recessive gene, the odds that this couple will have a child affected by Tay-Sachs are one in four with each pregnancy. All children with this disease die before they are five years old. As explained above, with each pregnancy there is a one in two chance that a child will be a carrier, and a one in four chance that the child will be neither affected nor a carrier.

There are a number of ways in which parents might find out the carrier status of their children. Couples who know they are both carriers and who have amniocentesis or chorionic villus sampling (CVS) to check on the status of their fetus for the actual disease will often be told whether or not the fetus is a carrier. Preimplantation genetic diagnosis (PGD) is becoming available for Tay-Sachs and many other genetic diseases. Thus, techniques such as amniocentesis, CVS, and preimplantation diagnosis, which are used to avoid having a child who will die of Tay-Sachs, will also yield incidental information about the carrier status of embryos and fetuses.[21] (Despite my arguments against automatically sharing information about carrier status with parents, I do acknowledge that parental knowledge of their children's carrier status may sometimes be an unavoidable concomitant of their right to decide which embryos will be implanted after IVF and PGD. For example, parents at risk for Tay-Sachs might produce three embryos through IVF and instruct the medical team to discard any embryos that are affected or that are carriers. The team would then need to inform them that all three embryos were carriers, and the parents might decide to transfer them all to the uterus anyway.)

Parents who have had one or more children before discovering their own risk might wish to take the whole family in for the simple blood test that can tell who is a carrier. Another possible route is through mass high school screening, as in the Montreal Children's Hospital Research Program, which tests tenth and eleventh graders in public and private schools with large numbers of Jewish students.[22] One can only speculate about the extent to which parents learn their children's status, but probably most parents know. Although parental consent is not legally required for children over fourteen in Canada, most schools exercise their prerogative of requiring parental consent for student participation. Although the students address the envelopes that will be used to mail the results and could have them mailed to a friend's house or pick them up from the school nurse, and although the screening staff would not divulge results to anyone except the students themselves, it seems likely that most students, naturally enough, will share that information with their parents. A counselor involved with the program told me that she thinks a lot of parents read their children's mail, anyway.

Despite the statement of the American Society of Human Genetics and the American College of Medical Genetics, that carrier testing should be "deferred" until adulthood, a survey of North American genetic service providers discovered that most providers had been asked to test adolescents for carrier status, and about half of the providers responded that they would test adolescents for carrier status for at least some conditions, including cystic fibrosis and sickle cell anemia.[23] Unfortunately, the study did not distinguish between older and younger adolescents. Geneticists who were most supportive of adolescent autonomy were most open to testing adolescents. However, without factoring in the elements of confidentiality and privacy, it is difficult to predict whether acceding to adolescent testing will actually afford the young person the most autonomy.

Just as adult clients of genetic counseling have powerful rights to privacy and confidentiality, so do children and even fetuses (if they will later be born). At first glance it seems preposterous to make privacy claims for a fetus, or even for a baby, whose parents will soon know every detail of its life—how often it eliminates, when it first smiles, and so on. But, assuming that this fetus or baby will grow to adulthood, there are privacy claims it can certainly make as an adult. Those claims will be empty if the information at stake has already been transmitted to the parents. Thus, geneticists who are considering a parental request for genetic testing need to make sure that they are respecting and preserving the child's right to decide, when he is an adult, what kinds of information he wishes to share with his parents.

It is difficult to talk about confidentiality between geneticist and young child, much less geneticist and fetus, as confidentiality implies a relationship in which one person shares private information with another on the basis of trust. And yet if this voluntary sharing of private information is not possible, how much more important it becomes for the professional to guard the privacy of those whose personal information is mined without their knowledge or consent. Such is the case when medical professionals are asked to discover and/or to disclose genetic information about children when discovery and disclosure are not necessary for the children's health and welfare.

Guarding children's privacy is especially crucial when the issue is testing children for adult-onset disease for which there is currently no available medical intervention, as in our discussion of HD, above, or for carrier status for recessive diseases. For these categories of genetic disease, probably the most important use made of the information is to make marital and reproductive decisions in adulthood. These decisions—whether to marry, whether to have children, whether to make use of controversial procedures to avoid genetic risk—are clearly within the child's most protected zone of privacy once she becomes an adult.

In the bulk of what has been written on privacy and confidentiality issues in genetics, the concern has been for the deleterious consequences of having one's genetic status known to possible employers and insurance carriers. But there are also important privacy issues to be considered within families. Sissela Bok describes confidentiality as resting on three premises: individual autonomy over personal information, respect for relationships among human beings and for intimacy, and the moral obligation engendered by making a promise of silence.[24] The third premise cannot concern us here, as the geneticist cannot make a promise of secrecy to a small child, let alone an embryo. But the first two premises do speak to this issue. The child will grow up to be an adult. Respecting her now as a potential adult means respecting her right and ability when she reaches that state to have control over information personal to her. Likewise, respecting her capacity as an adult to form intimate relationships (including sexual and marital partnerships) means respecting and protecting her ability now to decide then with whom certain secrets will be shared.

Choices and actions surrounding sex, marriage, and reproduction are perhaps the most jealously guarded zones of privacy in our culture. Our legal history reflects this high regard for marital and reproductive privacy not only in the highly contested abortion cases, but also in less controversial areas regarding contraception. In 1965, for example, Justice Douglas spoke for the Supreme Court in a case involving the right of married couples to purchase and use contraceptive devices when he described the "sacred precincts of marital bedrooms" and said, "We deal with a right of privacy older than the Bill of Rights. Marriage is a coming together for better or for worse, hopefully enduring, and intimate to the degree of being sacred."[25] In our religious heritage, the concept of the marital couple forming a new partnership distinct and separate from their families of origin is as old as Genesis, which says, "[A] man leaves his father and his mother and cleaves to his wife, and they become one flesh."

Recently, a number of scholars in bioethics have questioned the primacy placed on the individual patient as decision maker, arguing in different ways and from differing perspectives for a decisional ethics that pays equal attention to the family. Hilde and James Lindemann Nelson have talked about the institution of the family interacting with the institution of medicine, often with painful results.[26] John Hardwig has argued that decisions made by and for patients should take into account the impact that their continued care has on their loved ones.[27] Cynthia Cohen suggests that predictive testing of children can enhance family dynamics and bolster relationships. "The fact that members share the same vulnerability and the same information ... can lead families openly to air their concerns and options with one another as appropriate to their age."[28]

These are important and thought-provoking points. But I would argue that parental knowledge of their children's carrier status falls into a different—virtually unique—category, because of the use to which this information is put, that is, exclusively to make marital and reproductive decisions. When, in our Western culture, a person grows up, chooses a mate, and decides to marry, a new family is created. While the young couple retains significant ties to their families of origin, and may even live in the same house with them, certain bonds of loyalty and intimacy undergo a subtle but seismic shift. We acknowledge this in law and in the practice of medicine by automatically shifting the privilege and burden of making decisions for incompetent patients to the spouse as the new next of kin, even if the marriage is only a day old. One of the most common causes of marital strife is when couples disagree on how much of their "private business" is appropriate to share with their parents, or when in-laws are too intrusive and fail to respect the privacy and decision-making sphere of the new family.

Of all decisions for the new couple to make, perhaps the most intimate, and the most intrinsic to their status as mates who are "one flesh," are those connected with sexuality and parenthood. This is not to imply that the couple's parents have no interest in the matter. On the contrary, they are likely to have strong opinions and expectations about grandchildren, family size, behavior choices consonant with their religious and cultural traditions, and so on. But it is for the couple to decide together how their sexual and reproductive lives will be conducted, and ideally they will decide together whether and to what extent to bring their parents into that conversation. Whether the couple uses a condom or a diaphragm, whether they hope for one child or eight, or whether they would consider abortion for fetal indications are all decisions that belong within the privacy of the marital unit.

The Practical Implications

Let me illustrate my argument with a discussion of the practical effects of the dissemination of knowledge about the carrier status of a person at risk for Tay-Sachs disease. Although Jews are not the only ethnic group with a high risk for Tay-Sachs, I will use them as my example.

Someone who finds out that she is a carrier of Tay-Sachs disease has a number of options, all of which depend heavily on her religious beliefs and values. If she makes her discovery before she finds a partner, she could take her carrier status into account and take precautions against marrying another carrier. Within the Orthodox Jewish community, as we shall see, this is a common strategy. Of course, it could also be the case that this woman marries outside her ethnic community, choosing either a non-Jewish husband or one from the Sephardic group. But if her mate does turn out to be a carrier, a number of responses are possible. They could decide simply to take their chances and accept the hand fate deals to them. If they choose to take steps to avoid a Tay-Sachs baby, they could use gamete donation from a noncarrier donor. They could conceive, check on the fetus's status through amniocentesis or CVS, and terminate any pregnancy carrying a double dose of the gene. They could produce embryos through IVF, use PGD to determine which, if any, embryos carry both copies of the gene, and implant only the unaffected ones. They could choose not to procreate, either remaining child free or adopting. (Note that some of these options will garner information about the carrier status of unaffected fetuses, thus carrying the dilemma about parental information into the next generation.)

What is interesting here is that most if not all of these options are forbidden by the Orthodox Jewish understanding of halakha (Jewish law). Artificial insemination by donor is a matter of some controversy among Orthodox Jewish *poseks* (halakhic experts); many rabbis consider it adultery, others are not convinced that the child who results is legitimate, and many worry about the possibility of inadvertent marriage between half siblings in the next generation.[29] Abortion of affected fetuses is also not an option, according to most Orthodox interpreters, as halakha permits abortion only to preserve the life or health of the mother.[30] In vitro fertilization followed by preimplantation diagnosis might be an acceptable option, as some rabbis hold to the opinion that an embryo before forty days is "merely water," or that embryos have no status in Jewish law until they are implanted in a woman's womb.[31] On the other hand, IVF requires masturbation to produce sperm, and some rabbis frown on this even when procreation is the goal.[32] Deliberate nonprocreation is also not an option, as it offends the command to "be fruitful and multiply."[33]

Thus, from the perspective of many Orthodox interpreters of Jewish law, the only recourse allowed to the couple who discover after marriage that they are both carriers is to continue to procreate and to take their chances or to divorce. It is logical, then, that the Orthodox community, which already favors some form of matchmaking, has supported programs like Dor Yeshorim, in which young people of marriageable age are tested anonymously, and their status for Tay-Sachs disease and a number of other genetic conditions are entered into a computer bank by number only. When a person is considering marriage, she asks the other party for his Dor Yeshorim number and then calls the central bank and gives both their numbers. If neither or only one of the two people is a carrier, the caller is told that there is no impediment to the marriage. If both people are carriers for the same disease, the caller is advised "that another prospective spouse should be considered to avoid tragedy."[34]

The significance of Tay-Sachs carrier status varies widely with the beliefs and circumstances of the individual carrier herself and cannot be predicted on the basis of her ethnic identity or religious affiliation. We know that religious affiliation is a poor prognosticator of how people will make use of abortion and contraception, and presumably other reproductive strategies as well.[35] In the Montreal Children's Hospital Tay-Sachs screening program, where almost all of the clients are Jewish or Catholic, all but one carrier couple accepted amniocentesis, and all fetuses found to be affected were aborted at the request of the parents.[36] Now that there are many more options available to carrier couples, the number of affected children in the Jewish population has virtually reached zero. Since

2004, no child has been born with Tay-Sachs to a Jewish couple in North America. (This has the ironic result that more children are born with this disease in the general population, than in a population known to be at high risk.)

The carrier of Tay-Sachs disease may, upon adulthood, choose strategies very different from the ones endorsed by her parents and prevalent in her community. Her ability to make those choices may rest in part on her ability to control what information her family has. Thus, her right to make autonomous decisions is compromised, as well as her privacy and the privacy of the marital couple, by an earlier disclosure of her genetic status, when she was too young to consent. For example, a young woman may know that she and her husband are carriers and decide to make use of amniocentesis and abortion without informing others. This will be much easier if her carrier status is not known to others in the first place. Or the couple may decide to adopt and to allow their families to believe that they are infertile, when the truth is that they are using adoption as a way to avoid the consequences of their carrier status. Every genetic counselor would fiercely defend the right of this couple to make those decisions without consulting their families if that is their choice. And yet if children's privacy is not protected at an earlier stage, it is too late to go back and protect it when they are adults.

Another example comes from the documentary film, *Sound and Fury*.[37] The story follows a family with both deaf and hearing members. There are two brothers, one hearing and one deaf. The deaf brother married a deaf woman and now has two deaf children; the family is deeply committed to the deaf community and has refused cochlear implants for their five-year-old girl, even though she wants them. The hearing brother married a hearing woman who also has deafness in her family tree; they have just given birth to fraternal twin boys, of whom one is hearing and the other deaf. This couple also has an older child who is hearing. Conflict arises because the hearing couple decides to get cochlear implants for their deaf baby, a decision that causes a deep rift in the family. The deaf grandparents say they feel like they have been "slapped in the face," and wonder if the hearing couple still consider them part of the family. They worry that the little boy will grow up estranged from his grandparents. Interestingly, the existence of the two children born hearing in the young couple's family did not cause any tension; the rift occurred only because of the parents' decision to "convert" their deaf baby into a member of the hearing world.

Looking back, and depending on the young couple's other values, it may have made more sense for the couple to have had themselves tested for their carrier status, and then use PGD to avoid having a deaf child in the first place. They could have done this quietly, without consulting their parents, and avoided the deep conflict into which their family has been thrown. Even the inconvenience and slight medical risk of IVF and PGD might be offset, in some minds, by the time and energy put into working with their deaf baby so that he makes the best possible use of his implants. But again, this strategy would depend in part on the couple's carrier status being known only to them.

Our society, our legal system, and the medical profession give great deference to the privacy of reproductive decisions. It would be unconscionable for a health care provider to share information about an adult's carrier status with her parents; preserving confidentiality within families is an ongoing challenge and commitment for genetic counselors. Acceding to a parental request for testing, or divulging results of a test that was performed for some other purpose, violates privacy rights that will be activated when the child reaches adulthood. Why, then, would it be ethically acceptable to share that information with the parents of a minor child if it is information that requires a response only when that child is an adult?

Thus, at least as a rule of thumb, I support the conclusion of the Institute of Medicine's Committee on Genetic Risks that childhood testing is not appropriate for carrier status but that more research is needed on the appropriate age at which to undertake testing and screening for genetic disorders.[38] I also support the policy adopted by the American Medical Association that information about children's carrier status, if known, should be entered into the patient record, but discussion should be deferred until the time is appropriate, that is, when reproductive issues emerge. This information should not be disclosed to parents and should be maintained in a separate part of the medical record "to prevent mistaken disclosure." Further, it is crucial that physicians treat positive and negative results equally, so that individuals cannot infer what the results must be.[39] I do not advocate a rigid policy against acceding to parental wishes. Each family, and each genetic disease, has unique characteristics. But there is a special characteristic of carrier status that cuts across families and diseases: its unique importance for making marital and reproductive decisions in adulthood, and the extent to which those decisions are embedded in values generated by families, religion, and culture.

Newborn Screening and Genetic Knowledge

Routine newborn screening is another way in which parents and others can find out children's carrier status for a recessive trait. Newborn screening can also provide presymptomatic and predictive information about adult-onset diseases, or diseases that will appear later in childhood.

Although often conflated, there is an important distinction between genetic screening and genetic testing. Genetic screening tests a population to identify a subset of individuals at high risk for having or transmitting a specific genetic disorder. Genetic testing tests individuals who are already known to be at high risk, for predictive or diagnostic purposes. Thus all American babies are tested for phenylketonuria (PKU) as part of newborn screening. A Tay-Sachs screening program seeks to include all people of Ashkenazi Jewish and French-Canadian ancestry, because those populations are known to have a higher risk for Tay-Sachs than the general population. Genetic testing, however, would test a parent or sibling of a child known to have Tay-Sachs disease, or perhaps the sibling of someone known to be a carrier. Genetic testing could also be used to help clarify the diagnosis of someone who is already exhibiting traits of a genetic disease.

State-mandated newborn screening began in the 1960s by targeting PKU. In fact, in some places, newborn screening is still referred to as "the PKU test." PKU, as most Americans know, is a genetic metabolic disorder that quickly renders a child mentally retarded, unless that child is identified early and placed on a very restrictive special diet. Because early identification (before symptoms are apparent) is crucial, and because we have an intervention that can protect children from the ravages of the disease if it is identified early, PKU remains the "poster child" of a successful newborn screening program.[40] It is also a good example of the "rule of earliest onset," as in PKU the onset of the disease occurs in the newborn period.

For some time after PKU screening began, other tests were added in a very frugal fashion. In the past, screening for each new condition required a whole different test and different lab equipment. Given the tremendous expense of testing all newborns in a state, and the relatively small number of children identified, each new test had to surmount a rigorous test of its own in order to be adopted. That all changed with the invention of tandem mass spectrometry which allows for "multiplex" testing on the same blood sample for many conditions at once.[41] "Mass spec," as the insiders call it, has allowed for unprecedented expansion of newborn screening. Each state mandates a different panel and number of tests. An influential 2006 report by a working group convened by the American College of Medical Genetics recommended a panel of twenty-nine "primary" and twenty-five "secondary" disorders; these latter are disorders that would be detected incidentally while screening for the primary disorders. Today, every state does or soon will screen for between thirty and fifty-seven conditions.[42] A new technology is on the horizon: DNA-based microchips. Whereas "mass spec" measures levels of various metabolites in the blood, the microchips will screen directly for the genetic basis of various disorders.[43] The National Human Genome Research Institute, the home of the successful Human Genome Project, is currently working to reduce the cost of sequencing an entire human genome to $1,000 by 2014. "In 2007, the complete genome of geneticist and codiscoverer of the double helix James D. Watson was sequenced at a cost of about $2 million; in the fall of 2008, a company in California announced plans to begin offering complete human genome sequences for $5,000, starting in the spring of 2009."[44]

The explosive expansion of new conditions to be screened is controversial. When each condition had to be justified on its own, new screens were added sparingly. Now, there are many pressures to expand screening and no clear criteria for adding new conditions. One could think of this sort of like the national census: once you have put in place a huge army of people to ask a million households to answer a list of questions, every one with a research agenda or a cause to advance wants to add his or her question to the list. Advocacy groups, often made up of parents whose child might have been saved by screening from the consequences of a rare disease, push hard to add "their" disease to the screening panel. Interestingly, parents of children with disorders for which there is currently no medical treatment, such as Fragile X, are equally enthusiastic about routine screening.[45]

This explosive expansion of newborn screening has engendered a great deal of discussion as well as controversy. Underlying the discussion is the fact that almost all newborn screening is done without the informed consent of the parents. In many states, parents can theoretically refuse screening, but in fact as they are rarely told of it beforehand, or told only in very vague terms, this right to refuse is meaningless. Some ethicists argue that a test given without parental consent can only be defended on the grounds of potential benefit to children, backed up by strong evidence. PKU screening fulfills these requirements (assuming that the state follows up with parental education and makes sure there is access to the expensive diet), but screening for other conditions may not. Screening for cystic fibrosis, for example, has been controversial because not everyone agrees that there is a medical advantage to early, presymptomatic diagnosis. However, studies show that early diagnosis prevents malnutrition and improves children's growth and cognitive function.[46] A different concern has been expressed about Fragile X syndrome, the most common form of inherited intellectual disability. Although Fragile X can be devastating, one third to one half of all females with the mutation are intellectually normal. Identifying these children could cause unnecessary anxiety in parents or lead parents to have inappropriately low expectations of what their children can achieve.[47]

Everyone agrees that screening ought to result in a demonstrable benefit, but there is disagreement on what kinds of "benefits" count.[48] Again, there is no question that saving a child from the devastating effects of PKU is a wonderful benefit. But by what rationale should we screen for disorders for which there is no known medical intervention? Even if the infant itself does not benefit directly, one could argue that there are benefits to the family, or to society as a whole. Society, for example, could benefit from knowing more about the incidence of the disease. This, of course, is a research question, and normally we do not allow research on children without parental permission. Parents could benefit by having a heritable disease diagnosed early, before they embarked on another pregnancy. Parents (and arguably the child) could also benefit by being spared a "diagnostic odyssey" when the child does become symptomatic.

From some perspectives, there are few if any ethical limits on newborn screening. Duane Alexander, Director of National Institutes of Health's (NIH's) National Institute of Child Health and Human Development, considers the principle that one should screen only for disorders for which a treatment exists, as an outmoded "dogma." Alexander and others call for the development of multiplex screening that would screen newborns for "every medically significant genetic marker." Rather than demanding a rationale for adding a screen, every marker is presumptively screenable in the absence of a good reason to exclude it. The President's Commission on Bioethics terms this "newborn profiling."[49] In the 1990s, a number of reports argued that the only justification for newborn screening was the possibility of substantial benefit to the child. In the twenty-first century, that perspective seems to be losing out to a wider and not well delineated notion of "benefit" and of appropriate beneficiaries.[50]

There is not enough space here to follow these fascinating lines of debate about appropriate uses of newborn screening. For our purposes, it is important to note that, especially once the microchip DNA assay becomes the standard screening format, parents will probably routinely be told about their child's carrier status, even though it has no bearing on the child's health. In some cases that is already done. Newborns whose cystic fibrosis tests are "false positives"—that is, an initial finding of cystic fibrosis is not confirmed by a second, more sophisticated, test—are actually heterozygous carriers, something that of course their parents learn.[51]

Earlier I expressed some of my concerns about parents discovering the carrier status of their children as a corollary to amniocentesis or PGD. But the situation is factually different with respect to newborn screening. Where parents who know that they are at risk for, for example, Tay-Sachs disease, ask that their fetus be tested, one can make the argument that it is sufficient for them to know either that the fetus has Tay-Sachs or that it is healthy. Whether or not it is a carrier is something the child can find out for him or herself at the proper time. (It seems quite unlikely that parents would be interested in terminating a pregnancy due to the fetus's carrier status, as they would theoretically have to terminate three out of every four pregnancies.) In the newborn screening context, however, the parents themselves may be unaware of their own carrier status; thus informing them that their baby is a carrier (and that therefore at least one of them must be a carrier also) is crucial to alert them to their possible risk of having a baby with actual Tay-Sachs next time. In this context, therefore, my argument for guarding the child's future privacy must fall before the very real benefits of informing parents of their own genetic risk and the risk to their future children.

Direct-to-Consumer Genetic Testing

Moira Adams, thirty-seven, has recently been diagnosed with breast cancer. She is shocked but not completely surprised, as this disease is common in her family. Two of her aunts were diagnosed with breast cancer at a relatively young age; Moira's mother died of ovarian cancer. Two of Moira's cousins, women in their thirties, have been diagnosed with breast cancer. Her maternal grandmother died young, but no one knows the exact cause. Moira and her sisters Caroline and Susannah, along with their female cousins, have consulted a genetic counselor and have decided to be tested for the inherited alterations BrCa 1 and BrCa 2, which are often the cause of breast and ovarian cancer that "runs" in families and that tends to strike women before menopause. Caroline discovers that she is free of the alteration, but Moira and Susannah are not so lucky: they test positive for one of the alterations. This alteration confers a significantly higher risk of breast and ovarian cancer over one's lifetime, and possibly of colon cancer as well. Moira is coping with surgery and chemotherapy; the genetic results suggest that she should also consider removing both her breasts as well as her ovaries. Susannah, younger and healthy at this point, is wondering if she should complete her family soon and consider removing her ovaries and breasts. Both women are looking at a lifetime of increased surveillance: mammograms, colonoscopies, transvaginal ultrasounds and blood tests to detect ovarian cancer. Although the benefits are not yet known in women with BrCa 1 and 2, Moira has resolved to eat a low-fat diet and pursue a more active lifestyle. Caroline, meanwhile, while relieved at her negative results, is feeling "left out" of the family's current focus on the disease, and a bit guilty at getting off "scot-free." Last week, Susannah even lost her cool and yelled at Caroline that she wasn't "really" her sister the way Moira was, because they didn't share the same genes and the same fears.

Moira and Susannah have three children between them, two in preschool and one in kindergarten. Knowing that these children have a significant risk of having inherited the alteration, they ask the genetic counselor, Melissa, to begin the process of ordering genetic tests for the kids as well. To their surprise, Melissa gently tries to discourage them. Even if the children did have one or both of the alterations, surveillance such as mammograms would not begin until they were at least 18. Susannah accepts Melissa's arguments, but Moira is very upset. She counters that she is sleepless with worry over her two girls, and with guilt over the possibility that she "passed" the gene on to them. If one or both of the girls does have the alteration, Moira has a regimen of diet, sports, exercise, all worked out, and plans on making sure the affected child *understands the importance of having her children early. Because Moira feels disfigured as a result of her breast cancer, she also plans to counsel the girls to marry early, while they are still "attractive." Melissa is understanding and sympathetic, but she ultimately refuses to order the test for Moira's children, and her superiors back her up. Not to be denied, Moira surfs the Web and finds a company that tests for BrCa1/ 2 without involving a physician; she figures that, if necessary, she can always send the sample in and say the client is an adult.*

As we move into the twenty-first century, the power of the internet is eroding the role of genetic counselors as purveyors of information and as conduits to genetic procedures. Although nothing can replace the role of a geneticist in helping a person understand what specific genetic information can mean for her and her family, a great deal of general information is available on the web sites of NIH, advocacy groups, and so on. With the rise of direct-to-consumer advertisements for genetic tests, and testing being offered over the Web with little or no involvement of a physician or genetic counselor, the position of health professionals as "gatekeepers" is certainly changing. Some tests do require a blood sample, drawn by a phlebotomist, which would make it difficult to pass one's toddler off as an adult, but in most cases tests require only a cheek swab or saliva sample.[52] Had Melissa gone to DNAdirect.com, she would have completed a short questionnaire about her personal and family history, and information about her ethnic background. The site's algorithm uses this data to spit out recommendations for specific tests, which the consumer can then buy with a credit card. A kit is sent out, a sample returned, and the results made available to the consumer through a secure area on the web site.[53]

Although many health professionals are dubious about these sites and about the quality of counseling offered, consumers see a number of advantages. Perhaps the prime attraction is enhanced privacy and individual control of genetic information (and no fear that the physician will accidentally reveal genetic information to an insurance company or employer). Even in countries with universal health coverage, people may believe they have cause to fear losing their life insurance or paying higher premiums. A consumer's motivation to seek a test may be quite different from the protocol followed by a physician in deeming a test worthwhile. Although professionals may believe that a particular test does not have enough clinical significance, or does not offer any clear avenues of response if one does have the condition, consumers may have different motivations. We may well be approaching that very situation with regard to the test for the apolipoprotein E (APOE) allele, one form of which confers a greater risk for developing Alzheimer disease (AD). Most professionals believe that there is little point in offering the test, for a number of reasons. Alzheimer disease is a dreaded disease; those responses to a higher risk that might perhaps make sense (exercise, watching one's cholesterol and blood pressure) are things everyone should do anyway; plenty of people without the "bad" version of the gene do not get AD, while plenty of others who do not have the "bad" version do. While we know that, statistically speaking, one's lifetime risk of AD is higher if one has one or two APOE4 alleles, that's certainly not the whole story. So from many geneticists' point of view, there is no benefit, and much risk, in offering a test that gives no usable information. Consumers, however, may well have a sharply different perspective. They might put more faith in the efficacy of crossword puzzles to ward off genetic risk, or they might believe that they would be more likely to take charge of their cholesterol and blood pressure if they had a "scary" result. They might simply like to know their results, even if they are not definitive.

The web site Alzheimer's Mirror, hosted by the direct-to-consumer genetic testing company Smart Genetics, blares on its home page: *Knowing your Alzheimer's risk can empower you to make better decisions for your health, your family and your future. Call 877-xxx-xxx today.* For $399, a person can send in a cheek swab, along with personal and family information. Based on the person's age, gender, family history, and genetic results, a genetic counselor explains the risk assessment to the consumer over the phone. Although I suspect it would be quite difficult to find a geneticist who would knowingly do AD testing on a child, nothing in this process guarantees that the consumer writing the check and talking to the counselor is the same person as the individual from whom the sample was taken.

Thus, it is no longer enough to appeal to genetic counselors to protect the child's future autonomy by refusing inappropriate testing,. Parents themselves should think long and hard before testing children for any reason not directly related to the child's own health and well-being. A parent who has gone through the difficult decision to take a genetic test, ought to be aware of how many factors need to be sifted. Knowing one's genetic risk can change family dynamics, change one's sense of self, and possibly invite discrimination based on someone else's (mis)understanding of that risk.

The rule of earliest onset is helpful here. The reasons for following Kodish's rule can be grouped into two clusters. In the first cluster are straightforward claims of beneficence, that is, claims to benefit the child or protect it from harm. Possible harms from genetic testing are discrimination, stigmatization, and being pegged in the family as the "sick" child or the "problem" child. It distorts familial relationships to treat siblings differently from an early age because of their differing genetic status, when their actual health status is the same. In the second cluster are claims to protect the child's future autonomy and privacy, that is, her right to decide for herself as an adult whether or not to get tested (and with whom to share the resulting information). Kodish points out that genetic testing "may offer accurate prediction of future disease status," and that people with different value systems and different religious perspectives may hold sharply differing views about using science to predict the future, which some may see as "tamper[ing] with divine providence." Acting now to test children, based on the parents' values, forecloses the opportunity for children to decide for themselves later on.

Unlike genetic counselors, parents do not have a uniform code of ethics we can look up on a web site. In my view, the chief job of parents (beyond the basics of food, shelter, education, and love) is to raise autonomous adults who can make independent and thoughtful decisions. To do that, we must educate children and encourage habits of independent thought (while explaining why we hold the views we do, and why we think they are best). More than that, we must not unnecessarily preclude their adult decisions by foreclosing their options when they are children.

Genetic counselors and medical geneticists assiduously protect the privacy of their clients. They insist, as we saw in Chapter 1, that clients facing genetic risks have the right to make their own decisions based on their own values. Further, geneticists maintain that only the client can decide to share her genetic information with others, even when those others are family members with a real need for the information. There is no good argument as to why these values of autonomy and privacy should be focused on the adult clients of geneticists. Children, at least with respect to the adults they will become, also have claims to autonomy and privacy. Thus parental requests for genetic information about their children, when they have no immediate relevance to medical intervention or disease prevention, should generally be resisted.

Sex Selection

It was the monthly meeting of the Ethics Committee at Rubin Hospital for Women. Two dozen people spooned up their lunchtime yogurt and listened intently as the doctor outlined his problem and asked for guidance. An Indian couple now living permanently in America had been referred to him for routine amniocentesis because the wife, who was pregnant, was over thirty-five. Because fetal anomalies such as Down Syndrome are much more common with advancing maternal age, it is now standard practice to offer, even to urge, that older pregnant women undergo genetic testing that can detect the most common fetal abnormalities in time for the women to decide whether or not she wants to continue the pregnancy. Although this couple had been interested in testing for fetal problems, they also expressed their interest in knowing the sex of the fetus and their intention of aborting the pregnancy if it was a girl. They already had one daughter, thought that two children was the right size for their family, and came from a culture in which having a son was of great importance. The woman knew that her mother-in-law would view her as a failure if she did not provide her husband with a son.

The doctor felt that he was in a real bind. The couple had good medical reasons for wanting the amniocentesis; indeed, failure to offer amniocentesis and genetic testing to a woman over thirty-five years would be malpractice. There is no way to examine a fetus's chromosomes without immediately knowing what sex it is; the doctor could not blind himself to that information. Could he refuse to pass the information on to the parents? It would seem as if they have the right to know everything about the fetus that the doctor found out, and telling prospective parents the sex of the fetus is the common practice, but as the doctor said, "If that baby is a girl and I tell them that, I will feel as if I am signing its death warrant."

SEX SELECTION—the use of abortion or some other strategy to make sure that one's baby is of the desired sex—is a challenging ethical issue, especially for pro-choice feminists. Because they are pro-choice, they want to defend the pregnant woman's right to make reproductive decisions based on her *own* values, not on those of some doctor or lawmaker. But because they are feminist, they want to condemn a practice that historically has been used to prefer boys over girls.[1] As Tabitha Powledge has said, sex selection is "a perniciously sexist technology the regulation of which appears to me also to be perniciously sexist."[2] In this chapter, I sketch out some of the traditional arguments for and against sex selection. However, many of these arguments—based as they are on the preference for males and on the troubling moral status of abortion—are less and less relevant, at least in North America and Western Europe. So the bulk of this chapter addresses the more difficult problem: in the absence of abortion, and if as many prospective parents want girls as want boys, is there any reason to be concerned about the ethics of sex selection?

Sex selection through abortion has been available since the advent of genetic testing through amniocentesis in the mid-seventies, and in some countries, amniocentesis, or its much cheaper cousin, ultrasound, is widely used for sex selection despite efforts to make it illegal.[3] In the West, ultrasound and/or amniocentesis followed by abortion of the "wrong"-sex fetus certainly occurs, but nobody knows how often.[4] As the case at Rubin Hospital demonstrates, a couple can have more than one reason for desiring amniocentesis. Any couple can produce a plausible reason for wanting the test. If they are informed that the fetus is healthy and then go elsewhere for an abortion because it is not the sex they desired, who is to know? A new and unproven method of prenatal sex selection is a maternal blood test, when the woman is only five weeks pregnant, that can find specific male and female biomarkers. The woman pricks her finger, sends off the sample, and receives the results within 48 hours, for a total price of less than $300.[5] An even newer (and also unproven) option is on sale in drugstores in the United States and Canada: a urine test at ten weeks of pregnancy tells you the sex of the baby, with 80 percent accuracy, in the privacy of your home, for only $39.95.[6] These developments could revolutionize postimplantation sex selection, by allowing women to receive results privately, even anonymously, and to have abortions earlier.

In large part because of their commitment to respecting the autonomy of the client, a surprising number of genetic counselors are willing to assist clients in having a baby of the "right" sex, even if that means recourse to abortion. In a 1989 survey, a majority of American geneticists said they would perform prenatal diagnosis for sex selection or refer the patient to someone who would. (Fletcher/Wertz) A 2008 survey of in vitro fertilization (IVF) clinics of United States found that three quarters of them provided preimplantation genetic diagnosis (PGD), and of those, almost half report providing PGD for sex selection in the absence of a medical reason. Nonmedical sex selection was performed in 9 percent of the PGD cycles reported by clinics in 2005.[7]

Sex Selection and Abortion

To make the argument against the use of abortion purely for sex selection is both too easy and too hard. It is too easy because anyone who believes that the implanted human embryo has some moral status—that is, some claim to be taken with moral seriousness—believes that abortion should occur only for weighty reasons, of which sex selection is rarely a plausible example. (This belief, of course, is quite compatible with the belief that every woman should be legally free to decide the weightiness of those reasons for herself.) There are situations in which the reasons for sex selection do appear weighty. One reason would be where the prospective parents are trying to avoid the birth of a child with a sex-linked disease and, due to the imperfect state of genetic testing, can only discover whether or not the fetus is of the affected sex, and thus at 50 percent risk. Until recently this was the case with hemophilia, and it is still the case with some Duchenne Muscular Dystrophy mutations, and with a rare but lethal disease called Goltz syndrome.[8] In these instances, the fetus was aborted not because it was male per se, but because it had a 50 percent chance of having the disease. Thus, it was not truly a case of sex selection.

Another weighty example might be a married woman in a culture in which not producing a son would be a virtual death sentence.

There are still places in India, for example, where failure to produce a son is always blamed on the wife and may result in her being persecuted by her in-laws, perhaps dying from malnutrition or neglect, or, in the extreme case, being murdered so that her husband can remarry. But in this case the moral critique would focus on the unjust and immoral aspects of the culture this woman inhabits, and any arguments in favor of sex selection in her case would be a purely provisional argument embedded in a larger argument for changing the values of the society in which she lives. Barbara Katz Rothman, an unrelenting critic of sex selection, nonetheless believes that an Indian woman "who knows what faces her third daughter" and decides to abort is making a decision not unlike that of a woman who knows the inadequacy of the support system for the mentally disabled in our current society and decides to terminate a fetus with Down Syndrome.[9]

It is too hard to make the argument against sex selection by abortion because, as decades of bitter and largely fruitless debate have shown, if a person believes that an implanted human embryo has no moral status with no claim on our protection, there is no obvious way to persuade her otherwise. Many people in the American pro-choice movement appear to hold the view that there is no appropriate arena in which to initiate a moral critique of decisions about abortion. (In fact, it is probable that most pro-choice advocates do privately feel that some reasons for having abortions are more morally defensible than others. However, the political climate in the United States, where the right to abortion is constantly under attack, provokes a kind of siege mentality. Many pro-choice believers fear that any public discussion that suggests a moral condemnation of some reasons for abortion—of which sex selection is an obvious candidate—will open the door to the legal condemnation sought by advocates on the other side.)

Sex Selection Detached from Abortion

Fortunately, we do not need to settle the abortion question here, because my goal is to answer the tougher question: Is there anything morally suspect about sex selection if it could be accomplished *without* recourse to abortion? Due to technological advances in assisted reproduction technology, sex selection without abortion is moving from a theoretical question with practical importance for only a few people, to an option for middle-class couples.

From time immemorial, people have had theories about what causes babies to be male or female and have acted on those beliefs to try to influence the outcome of conception. Folk beliefs include putting an axe under the bed before intercourse to conceive a boy, hanging the man's overalls on one bedpost or the other, eating sweet or sour foods, placing the bed in a particular direction, and so on. Hebrew and Greek sages agreed that girl babies came from the left testicle and boys from the right; even into the eighteenth century French noblemen were advised to have their left testicles removed to ensure a son.[10] Medieval women ate rabbit testicles to conceive boys.[11]

More recent theories, taking into account scientific knowledge about conception, have suggested that timing of intercourse and using douches to change the acidity of the vaginal canal can at least influence the odds. However these strategies have proven to be of only limited success.[12] Other methods of selecting the sex of one's offspring are so unwieldy that it is hard to imagine a couple having recourse to them unless they were using them already for some other reason. A couple using IVF and genetic biopsy to avoid a child with a genetic defect might also choose to implant only male or female embryos (assuming they had enough embryos to choose from), but this strategy is too cumbersome, expensive, and risky to the woman's health to employ for sex selection alone.

Recently, however, a simpler method of sex selection has appeared. In September 1998, researchers at a Virginia fertility center announced that they had come close to perfecting a system by which sperm are sorted into those that produce girls and those that produce boys. We have known for some time that sperm carrying the Y chromosome (for boys) have slightly less genetic material than those carrying the X chromosome (for girls). The Virginia scientists capitalized on this difference to sort sperm into two groups. The process is far from perfect; MicroSort technology currently provides an average increase in X-bearing sperm to 88 percent in the enriched X-sorted sample and an increase of Y-bearing sperm to an average of 73 percent.[13] This is significantly higher than the roughly fifty-fifty ratio in natural procreation. The sorted sperm is then delivered to the female partner through intrauterine insemination. In their first announced results, thirteen of fourteen couples who wanted a girl achieved their goal; the result for boys was roughly similar.[14] At present, the process is quite expensive (at least $4,000 per cycle) and available only at two clinics operated by the Genetics and IVF Institute in Virginia and California. GIVF reports its pregnancy rate at 15.6 percent per cycle.[15] However, as with all technologies, there is reason to believe that costs will come down over time and access will become easier. "Should ongoing research eventually produce selective spermicides that would permit sex selection via natural intercourse, all such objections to the means would be much diminished or even disappear. We would be left to evaluate only the end itself."[16] Opponents of sex selection can no longer rely on arguments tied to the morality of abortion, nor can the risk and costliness of selection techniques buffer us from the necessity of grappling with the basic question: Is there anything ethically wrong with sex selection, in and of itself?

Population-Based Arguments for and against Sex Selection

One group of arguments against sex selection assumes that if parents are able to choose their children's sex, the world population will become skewed. Myriad studies support the long-held assumption that worldwide there is a strong preference for boys.[17] If true, a simple method of sex selection would lead to fewer women in the population. Some commentators think that this might improve the status of women by making them more desirable.[18] However, most scholars think that women would come to be valued primarily for their reproductive potential and would be forced into even narrower roles, kept in purdah, and so on. In the popular novel *The Handmaid's Tale,* Margaret Atwood imagines a world in which most women are sterile, and the few remaining fertile women are all virtually enslaved as walking wombs in the service of highly placed men and their infertile wives.[19] Perhaps a world in which there were relatively few women altogether might tend toward the same result. In a study that examined several modern and historical populations with dramatic sex imbalances, researchers found that such societies are likely to be characterized by great importance attached to female chastity, marriage at an early age for women, and women being regarded as inferior to men in judgment and political affairs.[20] In China, where the "one child policy" and son preference have combined to create a very skewed population, a "bride market" has emerged in which young women are kidnapped and sold into forced marriages in areas that lack women.[21] By 2020, it is estimated that the number of young "surplus males" unable to find brides could be more than 35 million in China and 25 million in India.[22] Sex imbalances could also lead men to look for brides among younger and younger girls, favoring the re-emergence of customs such as child brides and betrothals of children.[23] As Robyn Rowland has said, "Women are the most exploited, manipulated, oppressed and brutalized group in the world, yet we have the numbers. What would our status be as a vastly outnumbered group?"[24]

In many developing countries, startling gender imbalances already exist, caused by a combination of infanticide of female babies, abortion of female fetuses, and general neglect of female children. In the absence of any human intervention, the number of boy babies born would normally exceed slightly the number of girls, but girls, who are somewhat stronger at birth, have a better survival rate. Thus the average sex ratio at birth around the world is about 105 boys for every 100 girls,[25] what one writer calls the "biological sex ratio" rather than the "cultural" one.[26] Once these babies have passed their infancy, the ratio is about equal, with perhaps slightly more girl children.[27] However, in societies where boys are valued over girls, interventions such as prenatal sex determination followed by abortion, infanticide, or neglect can skew this ratio in dramatic ways. In India, for example, there are many reasons why boys are considered an asset to the family and girls a detriment. Boys remain with their families after marriage, thus adding to the communal labor pool. Girls go off to live with their in-laws, and their labor is lost. Furthermore, the pernicious, relatively recent custom of dowry, which began with the upper classes and has now seeped down to even the very poor, makes marrying off one's daughters an extremely expensive proposition, especially when one also considers the cost of the wedding preparation, which are borne entirely by the woman's family.[28] (A student of mine recently handed me a beautifully printed invitation to his sister's wedding, back in India. When I jokingly remarked that his parents would be quite surprised if I actually showed up, he responded that they probably wouldn't notice, as there would be over 2,000 guests.)

You might think that the result of these combined factors would be a group of unmarried women, who arguably could have contributed to the overall good of the family or of society by helping with child care, contributing labor, joining a religious order, or taking on traditional female roles such as nurse and teacher, but these options are not available in India (at least among Hindus). In the south Indian state of Tamil Nadu, one young couple explained the economic facts of life to journalist Elisabeth Bumiller. The husband made a dollar a day as an agricultural laborer, and his wife half that amount for exactly the same work. They had one little girl and a baby boy. In order to prepare for their daughter's wedding expenses, they had put $250 into a local bank savings program called the Marriage Savings Plan. This would appreciate to about $1,700 when the young woman was ready for marriage and would be used for her dowry. They would then ask for an equivalent amount from the family of the girl their son would marry. The couple explained that they had killed their second child, a daughter, at birth, because they could see no way to provide for her. Another deposit in the Marriage Savings Plan would probably have put them in debt for life, but without a dowry, their second daughter's life would have been untenable. The daughter would have been shunned in their community, and the father would have failed in one of his most important religious duties: marrying off his daughter. When one adds to this situation the fact that Hindus believe that only a son can light the funeral pyre of his dead parent, one sees the powerful impetus for avoiding the birth of "excess" daughters.[29] A Nepali woman told researchers:

> "I could not bear a son. God has punished me and will continue to punish me even after my death because there is no son to look after me in this state of mine and also no son for the salvation of my soul after the death. So I am a living dead."[30]

Although Bumiller found that infanticide was often used by the rural poor, who could not afford testing and abortion, feticide was common among wealthy women in urban area. Even if they could afford more girls, they bowed to social pressures that stigmatized women who had many daughters and few if any sons.[31] Other scholars remind us that while feticide and infanticide are powerful elements in the continuing loss of girls, the most significant decrease in girls occurs between the ages of one and four, due to widespread practices of favoring boys over girls in nutrition and medical care.[32]

The net result is that in many developing countries the sex ratio is becoming increasingly skewed. When one compares the number of girl children that would exist if boys and girls were treated equally with the number that actually do exist, one comes up with a figure of 100 million missing females around the world, according to Nobel prize-winning economist Amartya Sen.[33] In, China, a 1991 census found 93.8 females for every 100 males; that number was 92.1 in Pakistan, and 94.5 in Afghanistan.[34] Across much of the developing world, the trend is definitely for the worse. In India, for example, in 1981 there were 96.2 girls for every boy, but in 2001 that figure was 92.7.[35]

One might have thought that as women became more educated and as family planning and population control are more widely accepted in developing countries, girls would become more valued, but unfortunately the reality is more often the reverse. In societies where adults value small families, there is less "room" for excess daughters, and couples are even more likely to resort to sex selection to ensure that, if only two children are desired, at least one of them is male.[36] As Das Gupta and Bhat explain, when fertility declines, the total number of children that couples desire falls more rapidly than the total number of desired sons. "The difference in speed of these trajectories narrows the space left for daughters, and results in greater pressure to remove girls. This seems to have been the case in India during the 1980s, when total fertility fell by 20 percent, whilst the number of sons desired by women who did not have any fell by only 7.4 percent. A study in Punjab has shown that while educated women desire smaller families, their desired number of sons fell by only 20 percent compared with a 35 percent reduction in the number of daughters desired."[37]

Sex selection for population control is an especially potent argument when applied to developing countries. One version of this argument proposes that if there were fewer females in the next generation there would obviously be fewer "breeders," and therefore fewer children born, a boon in overpopulated countries that have had only qualified success with more conventional avenues of family planning.[38] A different version relies on the fact that in the absence of sex selection techniques, people often have larger families than they really want in order to produce the desired number of boys. Thus in India, giving people the opportunity to preselect their offspring would result in smaller families. Since societies that highly value boys and devalue girls tend to be the same societies as those struggling with high population rates, sex selection could have a powerful impact. Furthermore, sex selection by the sperm sorting method would be morally preferable to abortion and infanticide, and much less harmful to women's physical and emotional health. Against these arguments, critics assert that eliminating females to control population is inherently sexist, racist, and misogynist, and will not necessarily work.[39] If it is true that a society with fewer women will tend to restrict their societal roles, we may discover that—with only childbearing to define them—women in these societies will have larger families.

Another argument notes that the most effective strategy so far to lower the birthrate in developing countries is to educate and empower women, at the same time improving the infant and child mortality rate, thus reassuring parents that the children they do have will live to maturity.[40] If sex preselection provides a "quick and dirty" solution to the population problem, it may be doubly sexist—it eliminates the problem by eliminating women, thereby negating the necessity of improving their lives.

Interestingly, some developed but culturally traditional countries have moved dramatically from a preference for sons to a preference for daughters. In Japan, girls are now the infant of choice. Seventy-five percent of couples who plan to have only one child would prefer a girl, according to a 1999 survey. Only fifteen years previously, most Japanese preferred boys, but recent economic and social pressures on males are thought to account for the change. Also, girls are perceived as more compliant and affectionate, and easier to raise.[41] The same startling change has occurred in Korea. In a conversation with a reporter, Ms. Park He-ran, sixty-one years old, says that, as the mother of three sons, "When I tell people I have three sons and no daughter, they say they are sorry for my misfortune. Within a generation, I have turned from the luckiest woman possible to a pitiful mother." A generation ago, in this rigidly patriarchal society, producing a son was a woman's "paramount duty." As a result, Korea's sex ratio has gone from a peak of 116.5 boys for every 100 girls in 1990, to 107.4 in 2006. Factors contributing to the shift included changing economic conditions that favored women in the work force and thus made them more valued; a government campaign to change attitudes; and changing social mores caused by an industrial revolution in the1970's and 1980's. A primary reason for the all-importance of having boys was that sons, especially the eldest, were expected to care for their parents; sons supported their parents financially, and daughters-in-law cared for them in their old age. As in India, sons were security in the absence of a social safety net. The shift from an agrarian society to an industrial one, however, lured many men to cities, away from their family homes. Increased prosperity now allows older Koreans to put aside money for their old age. Married daughters, meanwhile, no longer "shackled" to their husbands' families, were freed to become more involved with their own parents, providing emotional and financial support, and were often felt to be better at it, warmer and more emotionally involved. Ms. Park said, "In restaurants and parks, when you see a large family out for dinner or picnic, 9 out of 10, it's the wife who brings the family together with her parents, not the husband with his parents. To be practical, for an old Korean parent, having a daughter is much better than having a son."[42] Meanwhile, a surplus of men in Korea is forcing bachelors to seek out wives in other Asian countries; marriages to foreign women tripled from 2000 to 2006.[43] In the United States, however, first generation immigrants from Korea, as well as from China and India, still show a preference for boys, at least to the extent that one child in the family must be male.[44]

Some Western scholars propose that in time the pendulum would come to rest in the middle, more or less as nature intended. One writer even suggests that if we started off with more males, the elderly population would be less disproportionately female, giving rise to better social opportunities in old age.[45]

A different version of the skewed-population argument focuses not on the status of women but on the effect on society. In recent presidential elections there has been lots of talk about the "gender gap" in voting, about Bill Clinton's appeal to "soccer moms," and about the differing political concerns of men and women. Women, not surprisingly, are more concerned than men on average about domestic issues such as education and health care, are more supportive of government spending on health and welfare, and are more likely to vote

Democrat. Sociologist Amitai Etzioni has suggested that because women commit fewer violent crimes than men, are more likely to attend church, and are more active supporters of cultural events, a world with proportionately fewer women would likely to more violent and less cultural, a sort of "Wild West" society.[46]

In North America in the twenty-first century, a skewed population does not seem a likely result of sex selection technology. In a 1990 study of 281 American undergraduates, only 18 percent indicated a willingness to use sex selection technology if it was "an inexpensive device or pill" that would allow them to select the sex of their first child. (However, of those who would use the technology, 73 percent preferred boys. It is also possible that if the question had been posed in terms of willingness to use the technology to select their *second* child, more people would have said yes but fewer people would have preferred a specific sex, reverting instead to "family balance.")[47] In a 1989 study Nan Chico surveyed 2,505 letters to Ronald Ericsson, a Montana physician who patented an early version of the sperm-sorting technique. Chico found that most couples interested in the process already had one child and were seeking "mixed" families. There was almost a fifty-fifty split in requests for girls or boys.[48] Ten years later Ericcson reported a larger number of requests for girls, despite the fact that his process (in contrast to MicroSort) has a higher success rate for producing boys.[49] MicroSort, which has a higher success rate for girls, reports that their clientele, perhaps because of that fact, are much more likely to want girls than boys. (MicroSort accepts only couples who have at least one child already and are seeking to "balance" their families.)[50]

Another piece of evidence has to do with parents who have two children of the same sex. For most of the past century, parents were more likely to have a third child if their first two were of the same sex, than if they had "one of each." That effect has lessened dramatically, presumably because parents care less about their children's gender.[51] A more fine-grained study of sex preference in the United States concluded that, in an "ethnically mixed" American population, there was no preference for sons among couples who were using IVF for gender selection, but that there is a strong demand for male children within some ethnic minorities, among whom the researchers identified Chinese, and Asian Indians. Caucasians and Hispanics, on the other hand, had a strong preference for girls in this study. Although this was a small study (and included only parents motivated enough to use IVF for gender selection in the absence of infertility) it does suggest that a large influx of immigrants from certain cultures might skew gender selection in the United States, if only for the first generation.[52]

A huge survey of over a thousand Americans from across the country discovered that participants, if given a choice, had a bias toward their first child being male. (This preference for first-born sons among parents expecting to have more than one child is pervasive, and has led some commentators to worry about the significance of birth order on personality; if many parents availed themselves of sex selection, would girls lose out on independence or ambition, by being more likely to be "little" sisters?) But when participants were asked if their sex preference provided they had more than one child, 5 percent wanted only boys, 4 percent only girls, 50 percent as many girls as boys, and the rest had no preference. Perhaps the most striking result was how few people were interested in sex selection at all. When presented with the hypothetical opportunity of influencing the sex of their children merely by ingesting a pink or blue pill, only eighteen percent thought they would do it. The researchers conclude that even the advent of a fairly simple type of sex selection technology is not likely to have a significant impact on the natural sex ratio.[53]

Another societal argument claims that if everyone were able to choose their children's sex, we would lose the lessons that come from having to make the best of the "wrong" gender, lessons that often lead to increased openness and decreased sexism. Barbara Katz Rothman speaks of how her father, not having had a son, was forced to make the best of it and take his daughter on fishing trips, and how those turned into her fondest memories of her father. Philosopher Michael Bayles uses the same argument to critique the desire for a balanced" family:

> One might reply that someone ... need not be sexist or irrational to want a boy. He has two daughters, and he would simply like to have a boy as well. Had he had two boys, he might have wanted a girl. But why would two daughters and one so be preferable to two daughters? Someone ... might respond that he would like a son so that he could have certain pleasures in child rearing—such as fishing and playing ball with him. But that too is probably a sexist assumption. As the father of two daughters, I have fished and played ball with them, watched my daughter play on a ball team, and gone camping and hiking with them, as well as cooked, cleaned house, done laundry and engaged in various other so-called women's activities with them.

Bayles concludes, "Were children allowed to develop freely their own interests and talents, children of the same sex would probably exhibit as much diversity as children of the opposite sexes."[54]

Sex Selection and Reproductive Choice

A common argument asserts that, whatever the causes and consequences of sex selection, choosing the sex of one's baby with available technology is part of a couple's basic right to reproductive choice. In a 1985 study, two researchers presented 295 American geneticists with the case of a couple who have four daughters and requested prenatal diagnosis so that they could abort a fifth pregnancy if the fetus was female. Sixty-two percent of the geneticists surveyed responded that they would accede to the couple's request. When asked why, the geneticists stated that they perceived sex choice as a "logical extension of parents' rights to control the number, timing, spacing, and quality of their offspring."[55] While most political energy has been focused on one's right *not* to procreate, by championing access to contraceptives and abortion, a great deal of scholarly thought has gone into the right *to* procreate, most especially the right to access new assisted reproductive technologies, such as the ones I discuss in this book. As we saw in the discussion of harm in Chapter 2, John Robertson and others argue that the principle of procreative liberty is strong enough to support parents' right to make any reproductive choices that do not bring a clear likelihood of harm to the child. In order to counter those arguments, therefore, one must focus on the possibility of negative consequences to the child.

The most common opposition to claims for the primacy of parental choice focuses on the dangers of turning children into commodities. Parents become consumers whose goal is the perfect child, with the assumed corollary that children who are considered to be less than perfect will be devalued. Thus just as yuppie consumers purchase the perfect house, the perfect pet, the perfect bottled water, they may also purchase the perfect baby. This is a theme we will see again in the arguments for and against reproductive cloning. Maura Ryan, in a feminist critique of unlimited parental choice, points out that assisted reproduction is expensive and burdensome; she wonders "how parents might look upon offspring when they enter the process with the belief that a certain kind of child is *owed* to them and after they have paid a high price for that child."[56] Some ethicists worry that if sex selection is accepted, the next step will be selection to avoid short children, nearsighted children, or children whose intelligence is merely average. Like the inhabitants of Garrison Keillor's mythical Lake Wobegon, we want to believe that "all our children are above average." The result could be a return to the excesses of the eugenics movement.[57]

Sex selection is the first instance of selective genetics for a "nondisease" trait. Whereas a "disease gene" causes a disorder such as Tay-Sachs, a "nondisease" gene causes or predisposes a person to a trait such as height, eye color, perfect pitch, or intelligence (assuming these are not in the subnormal range).[58] Bioethicists spill a great deal of ink arguing the societal implications of parents being able to choose children for traits such as musical ability or above average height, but the reality is that we're not there yet. Thus, sex selection is a fascinating aperture into our possible future.

Sex Selection and the Child's Right to an Open Future

Shira and Marty have been married for ten years and have three children. This was actually one more child than they had planned, but when their first two turned out to be boys, they tried one more time, at Shira's urging, to have a girl Their third child also was a boy. Marty would be happy to "stop while we're ahead" and enjoy their three healthy children, but Shira cannot give up her longing for a girl. Shira's own mother died when Shira was quite little, and her father raised Shira and her two older brothers by himself. He was a great dad, but Shira always felt that she had missed out on some of the "girl" things she would have enjoyed with her mother. When Shira and Marty received the amniocentesis results on their third child and discovered that it was a healthy boy, Shira was relieved there were no health problems but devastated at missing out once again on a daughter. "I crawled into bed and stayed there for hours, mourning my daughter. 'She'll never wear my wedding gown,' I blubbered. 'She's never read Anne of Green Gables.' "56 Shira and Marty figure that they can just manage to have one more child, given their finances and advancing age. Shira wants to enroll with MicroSort, a new company that will separate the X-bearing sperm from the Y-bearing sperm in Marty's ejaculate and significantly increase the chances that their fourth child will be a girl.

As I said earlier, the challenge I have set myself is to argue against sex selection in the absence of abortion, and in the absence of a marked preference for girls or boys within the culture. I believe that, even setting those considerations aside, there is a subtle but powerful argument to be made that sex selection is wrong because it is likely to abrogate the child's right to an open future. Why, after all, do parents have strong preferences for girls or boys, even if those preferences are merely in the context of "family balance," the one rationale that some ethicists are willing to find blameless, if not compelling?[59] (It is worth thinking for a moment about this concept of "family balance," so uncritically accepted by so many writers. Why is "balance" attributed to gender and little else? Is that because gender is the one attribute we can see immediately at birth, and also one of the few attributes—other than avoiding disease—that we can test for at this point? What do we mean by *balance*, anyway? According to the Oxford English Dictionary, balance is associated with stability, equilibrium, and harmony. Is my family unbalanced, disharmonious or likely to fall over, because I have one child, a son? Is my friend's family unbalanced because she has two daughters and no son? What about other sorts of balance? Should a family hope for one child who is athletic and another who is a klutz? One who is studious and the other who prefers to roam the outdoors? One who is a social butterfly and the other more solitary? Commentators believe that sex selection for "family balance" is not sexist because it does not prefer boys over girls and will not result in a skewed population. But it is still sexist to categorize a child primarily in terms of its gender.)

Parents whose preference for one sex or another is compelling enough for them to take active steps to control the outcome must, I submit, be committed to certain strong gender-role expectations of the children they will raise. As sociologist Barbara Katz Rothman points out, the genetic test selects for sex, that is, for a child with XX or XY chromosomes, but what the parents are really selecting for is *gender*, the social role of being a boy or girl, man or woman. When people go out of their way to choose, they don't want just the right chromosomes and the attendant anatomical characteristics, they want a set of traits that go with "girlness or boyness." Rothman says, "I've heard women say that they want the kind of relationship that they had with their mothers; they think they can't have that kind of a relationship with a son. I've heard women talk about wanting to have the frills, the clothes, the manicures together, the pretty mother-daughter outfits, the fun of a prom gown and a wedding gown, that come with girls."[60] Lisa Belkin, who surfed the websites devoted to discussions of gender choice, said that women who want girls "speak of Barbies and ballet and butterfly barrettes. They also describe the desire to rear strong young women."[61] If parents want a girl badly enough to go to all the trouble of sperm sorting and artificial insemination, they are likely to make it more difficult for the actual child to resist their expectations and follow her own bent. Rothman says, "When you start from the premise that one can 'determine' fetal sex in the sense that it can be chosen, then the stereotypes predict the choice: people who want an active, vigorous, achieving child will have boys. And when they want a sweeter, quieter, more loving child, they will have girls."[62] Rothman, one guesses, would not be especially pleased to discover that families in

Korea and Japan are becoming more interested in having girls; those families are still choosing on the basis of gender stereotypes.

Another concern is that parents who choose a child's sex will be less tolerant of children who turn out to be gay or lesbian. "The emphasis placed on 'family balancing'... in support of sex selection techniques also suggests that what is desired by families...is not primarily a child with different genitals but a child who conforms to the opposite gender role to the children they already have. ... Part of what is expected from sex selection techniques is a child that will conform to assumed (and desired) gender roles."[63] The mother who uses MicroSort to increase her chances of having a girl "who can wear my wedding dress," probably does not imagine that her daughter would don that dress to marry another woman.

Of course, it is probably impossible to raise children without some gender stereotyping, but the more we can manage to do so, the more we can give our children the gift of the most open possible future, the one least trammeled by notions of how girls and boys (and women and men) are "supposed" to behave. As feminist activist Letty Cottin Pogrebin says, "Instead of dividing human experience in half, locking each child in the prison of either 'masculine' or 'feminine' correctness, and creating two separate definitions of human integrity, the nonsexist parent celebrates the *full* humanity of each girl or boy."[64] The point holds even for those who would argue that gender stereotypes have been breaking down dramatically in the years since Rothman and Pogrebin wrote. Recent Olympic Games have featured exhilarating performances by female athletes; the U.S. Supreme Court has required the Citadel and the Virginia Military Institute to admit woman; West Point has had female head cadets and valedictorians; recent administrations in Washington have included a female attorney general, and female secretaries of state. But such optimism does not invalidate Rothman's point. If stereotypes are breaking down, why is it so important to have a child of the "desired" sex? If someone wants a daughter so that she can be groomed to be the first female navy admiral, that is still perceiving her primarily in terms of gender.

Because gender is only one among many characteristics, but one that carries very heavy baggage in our society, to view a child primarily through its gender narrows the child's ability to choose his or her own path through life. The same would be true (perhaps I should say, "*will* be true") if we could choose a child's height, musical ability, or aptitude for nuclear physics. At present, however, the one thing we can pinpoint and control is gender. Maura Ryan, arguing more generally against unfettered procreative liberty, challenges a framework where a desire

> [f]or a particular type of child ... is seldom weighed appropriately against the reality of the child-to-be as a potential autonomous human being. At what point does a being, who has been conceived, gestated, and born according to someone's specification, become himself or herself? And if a child comes into the world primarily to fulfill parental need, are there limits to what a parent may do to ensure that the child will continue to meet the specific expectations?[65]

Knowledge of Fetal Sex and the Child's Right to an Open Future

In the process of doing a chromosomal analysis to rule out Down syndrome and other problems, or in the course of a routine ultrasound, it is impossible for a lab technician *not* to determine the fetus's sex. The custom in the United States at this time is for this piece of information to be transmitted from the lab to the physician, who typically asks the couple if they wish to know the sex of their baby-to-be. Although women have reported mixed feelings on this subject, the vast majority of women who have had amniocentesis, CVS, or ultrasound do end up learning the sex of their fetus.[66] Because all women over thirty-five are counseled to consider amniocentesis, as well as younger women with medical indications or family histories of genetic disease, this means that a great many women in America today know their baby's sex before it is born. In fact, it is quite common for people to ask a pregnant woman whether she is carrying a boy or a girl, or for parents to announce their baby's name when he or she is still months away from making an appearance.[67]

Few commentators see this practice as an ethical issue (at least when parents have no plans to act upon this knowledge to abort a fetus of the undesired sex). It is certainly a strange development, in that it calls into question many common customs. Of course, friends and relatives will still be delighted to get that dramatic phone call from the happy parents telling them that mother and baby are healthy, but without the news that it is a girl or a boy, the announcement lacks a certain something. And the obstetrician does not say, as she holds the baby up for the mother to see, "It's a baby!" However odd these issues seem, we will leave them for anthropologists (and marketers of infant goods) to worry about.

In my view, there *is* an ethical issue here, albeit a very subtle one. There is some evidence to show that for parents who know the sex of their fetus, sexual stereotyping begins even before birth. Joan Callahan describes a conversation with a woman whose daughter had recently learned that the baby she was carrying was a boy:

> The woman had no discernible preference for a boy grandchild over a girl grandchild, but she was delighted to know that her grandchild would be a boy because, she said, she could now "begin getting ready for him."

When asked what that meant, she saw immediately that
it meant certain colors for blankets and sweaters, certain
sorts of toys and room decorations. Long before he was
even born, this child would be started on a "boy track,"
surrounded by blues and trains, never pinks and dolls.[68]

Pregnancy, perhaps especially when amniocentesis has freed one
from at least some of the attendant anxieties, is a time rich with
dreaming. If the fetus is quiet while one is listening to Bach, that
shows great musical talent, while every fetal kick means that an
Olympic soccer player is in the making. Just as the early developing embryo is totipotent, which is to say that each of its cells has an
unlimited capacity to differentiate into different tissues and organs,
so too the very early developing parent entertains a vast range of
possibilities. In our heavily gendered culture, many of those dreams
are lost and others become locked in the minute the baby is born and
the sex is known.

Most social scientists agree that gender socialization begins at
birth. Studies show that adults treat babies they think are male or
female very differently from the first day of life. Experiments with
babies from birth to a year show adults (men and women) interacting
quite differently with the exact same baby, depending on whether
or not they have been told that the (diapered) baby is a girl or a boy.
Based on the baby's supposed sex, they offered it different toys, spoke
in a different tone of voice, and interpreted the baby's behaviors
quite differently. (When "boy" babies cried, for example, they were
thought to be angry, while "girl" babies who cried were thought to
be scared.)[69]

These new techniques make it possible for gender socialization
to begin *before* birth. Barbara Katz Rothman, in an ingenious study,
asked women to describe the movements of their fetus during the
final trimester. Women who did not know their baby's sex before

birth used a variety of adjectives, without any pattern connected to the sex of their baby. However, when women knew their fetus's sex, a distinct pattern emerged. The movements of female fetuses were much less likely to be described as "strong" and "vigorous." The word *lively* was used often to describe females, but never males, although parents who did not know the sex of their fetus were equally likely to described male or female fetuses as strong or lively. Some masculine-sounding descriptions were used for female fetuses, but feminine-sounding descriptions were never used for males fetuses. This is in keeping with our culture, where tomboys are more acceptable than sissies and a girl in boy's pajamas looks cute, while a boy in a girl's nightgown sets off alarm signals.[70]

Thus it seems that knowing the baby's sex before it is born encourages the kind of gender stereotyping that threatens to limit the child's right to an open future. This is such a subtle argument that it hardly justifies frustrating parents' right to know should they demand access to the information. However, Rothman points out that the urge to know the fetus's sex often arises from the parents' awareness that the doctor or lab technician already knows. Rothman comments:

> It is not simply that the information is now knowable. It is also that it is known. It is known to the medical personnel, and once the sex of the fetus becomes part of the medical record, it makes sense to treat it just as one would other information on that record. Nancy said she asked the sex because: "I want all the information available to the physician to be available to me."[71]

One way to discourage the practice of reporting fetal sex while still respecting the rights of parents who insist on knowing is to adopt a policy suggested by Wertz and Fletcher in the context of discouraging actual sex selection. They propose that information about fetal sex remain in the lab and not be routinely reported to the doctor.

Therefore the doctor also would not know, and few patients would be prompted to ask for the information. The information would be available for parents who ask, but reporting it to parents would no longer be routine.[72] This would also avoid the now rather common occurrence of parents who have asked not to know accidentally being told by overenthusiastic nurses and physicians.[73]

Conclusion

Sex selection, even in the absence of abortion, raises serious concerns of justice in the context of developing countries and societies in which there is a dramatic preference for boys. But even in countries such as ours, where preference for boys may soon be a nonissue, I believe that sex selection presents an ethical problem because it promotes gender role stereotyping and encourages parents to invest heavily in having certain types of children. This combination of investment and stereotyping makes it more difficult for the child to grow and develop in ways that are different than, perhaps even in conflict with, parental expectations. Just *knowing* the fetus's sex, even outside of any attempt to predetermine it, may exacerbate gender stereotyping by allowing parents to begin the tracking process before the baby is born. Thus, policies that encourage sex selection or predetermination should be discouraged.

Cloning and Other Enhancements

6

Lorna and Jim Garcia met and married in their early forties. With their biological clock ticking, they wanted to have children as quickly as possible, but soon found that they had serious infertility problems. Lorna was approaching menopause and not ovulating regularly, and Jim's sperm count was low. Eventually, after many heartbreaking set-backs, the Garcias had a baby girl, Espera. When Espera was two, the whole family was involved in a car accident caused by a drunken driver. Jim was killed instantly; Lorna was not seriously injured. The baby was rushed to the hospital, where she was put on life support but pronounced brain dead the next day. Lorna, desperate to have another child that would embody the love she and Jim felt for each other, asked the doctors to save some of Espera's cells, so that she could some day clone them and have another baby genetically related to her and to Jim.

IN EVERYTHING THAT HAS GONE before, I have tried to avoid a "science fiction" response to genetic research and its applications. After all, today's science fiction is tomorrow's routine, as we can see from the common practice of casually asking pregnant women about the sex of their fetus. When Louise Brown, the first "test tube baby," was born in Britain in 1978, it was cause for tremendous hoopla and speculation. But the fact of the matter is, Louise Brown was the genetic child of both of her parents, who had merely used a little technical help to circumvent some blocked plumbing. Pretty mundane, from our point of view, thirty years later. Today I look out over the faces of my students and wonder how many of them were test tube babies.

In this chapter I try to bring the topic of cloning down to earth, debunk some of the sillier responses to the first scientific announcements, and see if the concept of the child's right to an open future can be helpful in sorting out the ethical issues of cloning humans. The reasons for this chapter are twofold. First, as cloning of humans is not yet being done, it is possible to take a deep breath and do some serious ethical thinking in advance of a scientific breakthrough, which is a rare luxury in the world of bioethics. Second, cloning is an over-the-top example, or perhaps the logical extension, of another problem in genetic ethics: the problem of enhancement.

The scientific advances in somatic cell nuclear transfer cloning (I'll explain that shortly) have come with amazing swiftness. In 1994, John Robertson spoke for most bioethicists when he said that cloning of mammals appeared "highly unlikely to be accomplished in even the midrange future";[1] in February 1997 Scottish scientist Ian Wilmut announced the birth of Dolly, the lamb cloned from an adult sheep. Animals that have been successfully cloned (that is, pregnancies brought successfully to term) include horses, cattle, sheep, dogs, cats, and others,[2] but in all these cases the ratio of attempts to success is extremely low, only about 1 to 4 percent.[3]

What exactly do we mean by cloning? There are two possible types of cloning, the first of which is really a misnomer. The first type is creating two, four, or eight embryos out of one original very early embryo. When the embryo is composed of only two to eight cells (called blastomeres), before it has begun to differentiate into the inner cell mass (which will become the embryo) and support cells (which will become the placenta), all the cells are totipotent which is to say that each of them has the ability to become an entire new organism. If one (carefully!) split a two-celled embryo into two, each of them could now become a new human embryo, and eventually a human child. Because the two children would have the same genetic material, they would, of course, be identical twins.[4] There is no obvious reason why one should not be able to produce quadruplets or even octuplets by this process; by splitting the new embryos, one could presumably go on splitting indefinitely.[5] This type of cloning (really quasi-cloning, as it does not involve creating a new organism from an adult of the species) created a mild stir when two researchers at George Washington University in Washington, D.C., announced in 1994 that they had successfully split some embryos into "twins" and had grown them for a short time in a culture.[6] Interest died down quickly, however, when it appeared that this technique had a long way to go before it could produce viable human embryos. As Ruth Macklin commented, "Perhaps the most sobering lesson to be learned from the announcement that researchers ... had performed this research on a human embryo is that scientific misunderstanding can generate unwarranted fears, spontaneous overreactions, and focus attention on wild and improbable scenarios even among people who ought to know better."[7] Following the dramatic debut of Dolly, the focus shifted to the second type of cloning, somatic cell nuclear transfer (SCNT). However, in January 2000 researchers at Oregon Health Sciences University announced that they had "cloned" a primate for the first time using the blastomere-splitting technique. After numerous unsuccessful tries, they brought to term a baby rhesus monkey.[8] Thus, before we leave blastomere splitting, it is worth looking quickly at some of the motivations that might drive people to use this technology.

Probably the most likely use of blastomere splitting is by couples trying to have a baby by in vitro fertilization (IVF) who have been able to produce only a small number of embryos. Because it is often necessary to go through more than one cycle before an embryo successfully implants and comes to term, couples try to have a number of embryos available and to freeze the ones that are not used in the initial attempt. Couples who can produce only two or three embryos might choose to use blastomere splitting to double or triple their embryo reserve, in order to increase their chances of successful pregnancy and to reduce the risk (and financial cost) to the woman of going through successive cycles of hormone shots and egg retrieval. In some scenarios, this practice could bring up some of the issues raised by SCNT cloning. For example, a couple could produce three embryos by IVF, and create another three by blastomere splitting (ending up essentially with three sets of identical twins). They freeze the cloned embryo of each pair and transfer the original embryos to the uterus, resulting eventually in one healthy baby girl. Five years later the little girl is killed in an accident. The parents want to have another child and, returning to their cache of stored embryos, decide to gestate the genetic twin of the dead child, hoping to "replace" their dead daughter. (Or perhaps they don't choose that result but simply transfer all three frozen embryos, and the only one that implants is their daughter's genetic twin.) Now we have the same situation as the one that concerns many people about SCNT cloning: a child growing up in the shadow of an older identical twin.

Other reasons for blastomere splitting might include having an identical twin "in reserve" as an organ or marrow donor for an existing child, a more efficient tack than the chancy process followed by the Ayala parents, who reversed a vasectomy to produce a little sister for an older daughter dying of leukemia, who was desperate for a bone marrow donor. The Ayalas had only a one in four chance of their new baby being a match for their older daughter, and even then the match was not as perfect as an identical twin would have been.[9]

The second type of cloning, and the one on which I will concentrate here, is SCNT. A somatic cell is any cell in your body other than sperm or eggs. Somatic cells have the full complement of chromosomes, half from your mother, half from your father. But germ cells (sperm and eggs) have only half that number (otherwise, when they came together in fertilization, there would be twice the correct number). In SCNT, the genetic material is scooped out of an egg cell and replaced with the genetic material of a "regular" or somatic cell, taken from anywhere in the donor's body. Thus, SCNT results in an embryo with a single genetic parent, unlike sexual reproduction, which always needs a male and a female. (Another way of looking at this is that the embryo does have two genetic parents–the mother and father of the donor. Thus, the genetic parents of the cloned person are also his or her social grandparents.) Rather than mixing up the genetic material of two parents to create a unique new individual, SCNT cloning results in an embryo that is virtually the identical genetic twin to the person—call him or her the "donor"—whose somatic cell was used.* The donor could, of course, be the prospective mother or father, or a stranger, as in our current practice of anonymous sperm donation, or a family friend or famous person or, presumably, someone now dead whose cells have been preserved.

---

* I say a "virtual" genetic twin because some genetic material is carried in the mitochondria found in the cytoplasm of the egg, which will slightly alter the DNA of the clone from that of its donor.

Thus, the two most salient facts about SCNT cloning are, first, that it is asexual, requiring only one genetic "parent," and, second, that the donor can be an adult. Blastomere splitting, as we saw above, requires that the cells of the donor still be in the totipotent stage, so that the only possible clones are very early embryos. (In both cases, of course, the developing embryo will need to be carried to term in a woman's uterus.) Although a number of mammals have been successfully cloned, so far there has been no success with primates. Even the "success" with domestic animals defines "success" in a very minimalist way; Hyun and Jung argue that the fact that fewer than 4 percent of cloned embryos survive to birth, and many of those with abnormalities, is due not to human error, but in "biological fact," with the implication that truly successful mammalian cloning may never be possible. Some scholars believe that SCNT cloning is incapable of producing a viable embryo when used on primate eggs.[10]

The announcement that Scottish scientists, led by Dr. Ian Wilmut, had cloned a sheep they chose to name Dolly tapped into an extraordinary reservoir of hopes, fears, and misconceptions. The hopes were expressed in such touching sentiments as that of the man who showed up at the Central Park memorial service for the late Princess Diana with a sign proclaiming *Clone Diana*. "I love her," he said. "To have another one of her, it would be a good thing."[11]

Most of the immediate reaction, positive or negative, seemed to share this man's misconception that the cloned individual would spring from the laboratory fully grown, rather than emerging from a womb as an unremarkable neonate. Many commentators seemed to forget that the genetic blueprint is only part of a person's makeup, mixing with the totality of experience to create a unique individual. (In Leon Kass's memorable phrase, they seem to confuse cloning with Xeroxing.)[12] Jean Bethke Elshtain, normally a thoughtful writer, blunders into one conceptual hole after another as she paints a nightmare of "a veritable army of Hitlers," against whom "an equal number of Mother Teresas would probably not be a viable deterrent."[13] Assuming that a baby born with Hitler's genetic makeup would also exhibit Hitler's beliefs, character, and personality is, in fact, to echo the very worst of Hitler's own genetic determinism.[14] Even if we stick to physical rather than psychological results, genes are not the whole story. To use a rather trivial example, some critics of blastomere splitting to create twins gestated decades apart commented, "You may not want to know, at 40, what you will look like at 60."[15] But when one takes into account eating habits, sports, hobbies, occupation, exposure to disease, number of children, and time spent in the sun, one immediately sees that two people with the same deoxyribonucleic acid (DNA) might look very, very different from each other at forty or sixty.

Upon sober reflection, it is obvious that cloning will not be useful to, say, create three more Albert Einsteins to meet a sudden nuclear threat, or a hundred Mother Teresas to make the world a kinder and gentler place. Nor will cloning create a species of demihumans whom we can keep in the closet until needed. Elshtain claims that "the cloned entities are not fully human" and therefore do not need to be treated with the same respect as the rest of us.[16] But that statement is baseless. The newborn baby who results from cloning is gestated and born in the usual way and is genetically as fully Homo sapiens as you, me, or Elshtain. Yes, the baby is the "'delayed' genetic twin" of an already born human, but there is no reason to consider it less than fully human in a legal or social sense, when we do not question the full humanity of genetically identical twins. Perhaps Elshtain's concern is based upon the fact that the cloned newborn would begin life as a laboratory creation. But that is equally true of babies conceived through IVF or intracytoplasmic sperm injection, and we have no concerns about their full humanity. Even the

Roman Catholic Church, which has been adamant in its rejection of almost all assisted-reproduction techniques, has never for a moment suggested that the children created through those techniques have any different status in the human community.

What, then, are the real ethical problems with cloning humans? Presumably, as in other forms of assisted reproduction, a technique as expensive and cumbersome as cloning will never become the norm. In vitro fertilization, the focus of so much concern when Louise Brown was first born, accounted for about 1 percent of babies born in 2005, according to the Centers for Disease Control. As Barbara Katz Rothman says, babies still wet their diapers and kids still need help with their homework; "the social order has not particularly changed."[17] Where is the ethical concern if an occasional couple, perhaps already precluded for medical reasons from procreating in the old-fashioned way, decides to avail themselves of cloning? Focusing on practical issues and staying away from the metaphysical, is there a foreseeable risk to the child born of such a procedure? Such a risk, if we can articulate it coherently, can form the basis of a judgment to go slowly and with caution.

Let me begin by sorting out two different kinds of motivations would-be parents might have for resorting to cloning. (Here I am concentrating on the SCNT variety, that is, asexual cloning from a cell taken from another person's body.) The first motivation I will call logistical. For some reason, this couple is having a very difficult time procreating, and cloning offers some unique advantage to them. The first two examples in chapter 4 ("Ethical Considerations") of the National Bioethics Advisory Commission's report on cloning are instances of couples who wish to make use of cloning for logistical reasons:

> A couple wishes to have children, but both adults are carriers of a lethal recessive gene. Rather than risk the one in

four chance of conceiving a child who will suffer a short and painful existence, the couple considers the alternatives: to forgo rearing children; to adopt; to use prenatal diagnosis and selective abortion; to use donor gametes free of the recessive trait; or to use the cells of one of the adults and attempt to clone a child. To avoid donor gametes and selective abortion, while maintaining a genetic tie to their child, they opt for cloning.

A family is in a terrible accident. The father is killed, and the only child, an infant, is dying. The mother decides to use some cells from the dying infant in an attempt to use somatic cell nuclear transfer to create a new child. It is the only way she can raise a child who is the biological offspring of her late husband.

I call these logistical motivations because the parents' goal here is simply to have a child. The duplicative element of cloning is a side effect, perhaps even one they would avoid if they could. The parents see cloning as the best option from an array of choices: adoption, childlessness, or reproduction with the use of a third party. If we would support the reproductive efforts of these would-be parents without cloning (e.g., if the infant in the second scenario had been conceived through IVF and the parents had saved a frozen embryo that could now be thawed and implanted), then the additional factor of cloning should not necessarily doom them in our eyes. Cloning brings in new problems and requires additional counseling, but it is not inherently immoral, nor is there a strong likelihood of harm to the child.

One group that might welcome cloning for logistical purposes are lesbian couples. One member of the couple could provide the DNA, and either she or her partner could provide the egg and its attendant mitochondrial DNA, and the other woman could gestate the baby. Thus, they would have created a baby that was truly the result of their joint biological effort. For same-sex couples who wish to have children, recent advances in the law have pulled in two directions. On the one hand, in Western Europe, Canada, and increasingly in the United States, gays have been granted the right to marry or to form civil unions that parallel marriage. This legal support for their relationship makes it easier to have children, because it solves all sorts of problems about guardianship, employee benefits, and so on. But for couples looking to create families through sperm donation, a combination of laws and societal mores are making anonymous sperm donation more complicated. In the United Kingdom, for example, all children born of gamete donation now have the right to receive contact information about the donor, when the child reaches eighteen. In Europe, the child's interest in knowing her origins is gaining legal acknowledgement as "a full-blown *right to know*."[18] So for lesbian couples who wish to procreate without inviting a stranger into their family, who wish to keep their parental dyad exclusive in the same way as heterosexual couples, cloning could be an attractive option. Theologian Karen Lebacqz argues that, if procreative liberty is indeed an important right, then justice requires the state to treat reproductive cloning, which allows lesbian couples to create a child with their own genetic material, in the same way that it treats IVF and other techniques that allow heterosexual couples to do the same.[19] Legal scholar David Orentlicher makes a parallel point from a different perspective. Given the string of Supreme Court cases that protect parents' right of privacy and autonomy over their families, including their right to control who is part of their family and who has access to their children, cloning is the reproductive technology with the strongest claim to constitutional protection, for gay or straight couples.[20]

In contrast, with duplicative motivations it is the genetic replication itself that is the attraction. Some duplicative motivations will not survive exposure to the facts; parents who think they can guarantee a saintly child if they could only get hold of Mother Teresa's

CLONING AND OTHER ENHANCEMENTS

DNA are clearly mistaken. Other duplicative motivations are less obviously foolish but more obviously perilous to the child herself. When parents, for example, wish a new, genetically identical child to "replace" a dearly beloved child who has died young, the psychological pitfalls are clear. No child could possibly live up to such glorified expectations, and the parents are likely to be frustrated and disappointed that the "new" child is so different. After all, the second child's experience will be dramatically different from that of her dead sibling, if only because the second child is a younger sibling in a family that has sustained such a tragedy. Thus, it is obvious, first, that the parental motivations are based on a mistaken notion of the importance of genetics over environment and, second, that the enterprise is almost certainly doomed to disaster. Health professionals should not find it difficult to refuse to participate in such an endeavor, especially when the couple that wishes to use cloning for duplicative motivations is still able to procreate in other ways.

Another duplicative motivation for cloning involves creating a second human being to provide a "spare part" for a sick family member, as in the third example of National Bioethics Advisory Commission report:

> The parents of a terminally ill child are told that only a bone marrow transplant can save the child's life. With no other donor available, the parents attempt to clone a human being from the cells of the dying child. If successful, the new child will be a perfect match for a bone marrow transplant, and can be used as a donor without significant risk or discomfort. The net result; two healthy children, loved by their parents, who happen to be identical twins of different ages.

To many people this is the most obnoxious motive for cloning. But as the example's last sentence suggests, it may not be as problematic as it appears. A child created by cloning will be a human individual with the same call on the protection of her family, the medical profession, and the state as a child conceived in the usual way. There is no reason to fear that she will be exploited any more (or less) than when existing children are good matches for their needy siblings. Our unease stems from the concern that the new child is being created only as a source of spare parts, that is, only as a means to someone else's end. This couple did not necessarily want another child; they wanted this child for this purpose. This very concern surfaced in the public controversy over the Ayala family, mentioned earlier, who conceived one daughter in the hope that she would be a bone marrow donor for their existing daughter. But as Thomas Murray points out, the Kantian dictum at issue here is that one should never treat other persons as means only, to the exclusion of treating them as ends in themselves. Given the many and varied reasons why parents choose to have children, as long as the new baby will be loved and nurtured for her own sake it is not ethically problematic to create her at least partially in the hope that she will be of use to someone else.[21] (How often have we heard parents say that they are planning a second child because they do not want their first child to be an "only"?) This is one of the two situations in which Jewish ethicist Rabbi Moshe Tendler would consider cloning to be acceptable (the other would be when a Holocaust survivor was sterile and cloning was the only way she or he could produce descendants). Tendler says that a child who was produced to provide lifesaving bone marrow for a sibling "would then be doubly loved."[22] Also under the heading of duplicative motivation, the most difficult case to argue against—on a factual basis—is when parents are focused upon a particular set of physical characteristics. Unlike the parents who wish to replicate Mother Teresa or a dead child, it is not as immediately obvious that the parents who wish to have an Olympic swimming star for a son are laboring under a mistaken notion if they want to buy and use a few cells scraped from the cheek of Michael Phelps. While certain genetic characteristics are not sufficient to be a top swimmer, they are surely necessary. In some fields (classical ballet, for example) only a very narrow range of body types is compatible with success. All the talk about the importance of nurture as well as nature cannot obscure the fact that, as John Robertson comments, "[t] he desire to clone arises precisely because genes are viewed as highly important, if not crucial, in making people who they are."[23] To quote conservative critic Leon Kass:

> Since the birth of Dolly, there has been a fair amount of doublespeak on this matter of genetic identity. Experts have rushed in to reassure the public that the clone would in no way be the same person, or have any confusions about his or her identity. ...they are pleased to point out that the clone of Mel Gibson would not be Mel Gibson. Fair enough. But one is shortchanging the truth by emphasizing the additional importance of the intrauterine environment, rearing and social setting: genotype obviously matters plenty. That, after all, is the only reason to clone, whether human beings or sheep. The odds that clones of Wilt Chamberlain will play in the NBA are, I submit, infinitely greater than they are for clones of Robert Reich.[24]

But assuming that parents understand that prowess in basketball or ballet depends on much more than just genetic inheritance, where is the harm in trying? The harm, I think, lies in the radical way in which cloning for these kinds of duplicative motivations limits the child's right to an open future, because it violates the child's nascent autonomy and narrows the scope of her choices when she grows up. Philosopher Hans Jonas saw this quite presciently in 1974, in a book entitled *Philosophical Essays: From Ancient Creed to Modern Man*. What bothers Jonas about cloning is that it destroys the clone's ignorance about his biological destiny and therefore endangers his "unprejudiced selfhood."[25] "Ignorance," says Jonas, "is here the precondition of freedom."[26]

> It is all a matter much more of supposed than real knowledge, or opinion than truth. Note that it does not matter one jot whether the genotype is really, by its own force, a person's fate: it is made his fate by the very assumptions in cloning him, which by their imposition on all concerned become a force themselves. It does not matter whether replication of genotype really entails repetition of life performance: the donor has been chosen with some such idea, and that idea is tyrannical in effect. It does not matter what the real relation of "nature and nurture," of genetic premise and contingent environment is in forming a person and his possibilities: their interplay has been falsified by both the subject and the environment having been "primed."[27]

Jonas concludes that the clone has been "robbed of the freedom that only under the protection of ignorance can thrive; and to rob a human-to-be of that freedom deliberately is an inexpiable crime that must not be committed even once." He enjoins us to "respect the right of each human life to find its own way and be a surprise to itself."[28]

Although Jonas's passionate language makes it appear that he is opposed to all sorts of human cloning for any motivation, he actually seems to leave room for what I have called logistical motivations. Jonas admits that "random cloning from ... anonymous and insignificant" donors would escape his major objections.[29] He does not see why anyone would wish to do it, but twenty-five years later, we can easily imagine infertile or genetically compromised couples who use cloning simply to avoid problematic aspects of adoption or gamete donation. Although these couples would not avoid the problem of knowing the history of the donor, they at least did not choose cloning in order to maximize the possibility that the child would echo the donor in some significant fashion. Thus, if it is done in a thoughtful manner, there seems no reason to condemn cloning for these motivations. However, where prospective parents enter the cloning endeavor from duplicative motivations, I share Jonas's unease (if not his certainty). Thus I believe that most duplicative reasons for cloning are unethical and ought to be discouraged.

There are three obvious objections to my claim here. The first is that everyone is born with one genetic inheritance or another—no one can simultaneously have the possibility of being a great football player and a great jockey. Those limits on our choices are simply the stuff of life; what difference does it make if one is very tall as a result of being cloned or as a matter of chance? The second objection is one I have discussed in Chapter 1, voiced by critics such as Ronald Green, that parents constantly influence or even pressure their children into playing out parental dreams; some of us might find that worthy of criticism, but not to the extent that our criticism drives public policy. John Robertson makes this argument when he admits that "abuses" of parental autonomy can occur, as when the Little League father expects his son to be a baseball star, despite the child's lack of interest, but he concludes that "our traditions of parental and family autonomy give parents wide discretion in rearing children that allows them to mold their children to their own ideas."[30]

The answer to both types of objections is the same. True, everyone is born with a genetic inheritance that enables some choices and not others, and true, parents are often quite assertive in their drive to influence their children's life choices. But allowing parents to clone children for this purpose elevates the problem to a new level. Ordinarily parents may wish for a daughter who looks like ballerina Suzanne Farrell and dream that she will have a similar success, but their wishes are tempered by the reality that reproduction is a crap-shoot and that the only predictable thing about parenthood is that it will be surprising. The chief charm of *The Fantasticks*, Off Broadway's longest-running production, is its rueful celebration of the mysteries of parenthood. The two fathers in the play, ardent gardeners, lament the unpredictable nature of their offspring in the wonderful duet "Plant a Radish":

> Every turnip green, every kidney bean,
> Every plant grows according to its plot.
> But with progeny, it's hodge-podgeny,
> For as soon as you think you know what you've got—
> It's what they're not.[31]

Expectant parents may interpret every intrauterine bounce as an incipient plié, but they know in their hearts that they can only keep their fingers crossed. In contrast, parents who take expensive, cumbersome steps to provide their child with a specific DNA in order to maximize the chances of success in a particular field will, I suspect, find it almost impossible to accept if the child hates ballet or basketball and chooses the life of an accountant or tympani player. As Leon Kass puts it, "[I]f most parents have hopes for their children, cloning parents will have expectations."[32] Parents will be focused, from the child's first days, on such a narrow range of possibilities that the child's right to an open future, her chance to explore her own options and interests, will be radically compromised.

A third objection to my argument is put forward by Dan Brock and relies on an issue I have already touched on: the fact that one's genetic inheritance is only one of many determinants of one's future. Brock writes:

> The central difficulties in these appeals to a right either to ignorance or to an open future is that the right is not violated merely because the later twin is likely to believe that

his future is already determined, when that belief is clearly false and supported only by the crudest genetic determinism. If we know the later twin will falsely believe that his open future has been taken from him as a result of being cloned, even though in reality it has not, then we know cloning will cause the twin psychological distress, but not that it will violate his right. Jonas's right to ignorance, and Feinberg's right of a child to an open future, are not violated by human cloning.[33]

But against Brock, I think Jonas's point is well taken—what matters is what parents (and the child herself) *believe* about the importance of genetics. If parents, however unwisely, believe that their son will certainly become a major football star and therefore they put aside no money for his college education and care only that his grades achieve the bare minimum, they have narrowed the scope of his future in ways Jonas and I agree would be immoral (and this point holds true whether or not their son makes it as a football star). Søren Holm makes this point a little bit differently, in what he calls "the life in the shadow argument."[34] Holm asserts:

> There is no doubt that the common public understanding of the relationships between genetics and psychology contains substantial strands of genetic essentialism, i.e., the idea that the genes determine psychology and personality. ... Therefore, it is likely that the parents of the clone will already have formed in their minds a quite definite picture of how the clone will develop, a picture that is based on the actual development of the original. This picture will control the way they rear the child.[35]

Further, Holm insists that "[i]t is important to note that the 'life in the shadow' argument does not rely on the false premise that we can make an inference from genotype to (psychological or personality) phenotype, but only on the true premise that there is a strong public tendency to make such an inference."[36] Again, we can soften Holm's critique by paying attention to the reason parents choose to have a child by cloning. If their reasons are purely logistical, it is possible that the careful counseling and screening advocated by Robertson and others will make the "life in the shadow" problem just one of the major issues any parents have to face, but not serious enough to ban the practice of cloning entirely. But if the reasons are duplicative, then their decision to clone should wither if they truly understand the information counselors are trying to give.

This distinction between logistical and duplicative motivations is also useful in thinking about a common concern expressed about reproductive technology: that it leads to "commodification." Commodification, as the National Bioethics Advisory Commission report observes, involves "treating persons ... as a thing that can be exchanged, sold, or bought in the marketplace."[37] This is a general concern about reproductive technology, where people worry that children will be turned into "products," gametes into "vendible objects," and women into "baby machines."[38] The concern in the cloning or genetic enhancement context is, I think, the same one that has been expressed since the beginning of our successes in providing parents with some modicum of control over the genetic inheritance of their offspring: that the children themselves will be viewed as "consumer products," much like other things that we order to our specifications and then return to the store if they are disappointing or defective. Many ethicists have feared a progression that begins with enabling parents to discover major genetic anomalies such as Down syndrome (and to decide whether or not to terminate such a pregnancy), goes on to test for relatively minor conditions such as cleft palate, and ends with encouraging parents to choose the sex, IQ, coloring, talents, and athletic propensities of their offspring.

Commodification is a more plausible concern when parental motivations for cloning are duplicative than when they are logistical. Parents who seek to clone for logistical reasons simply want a child, any child (or, to be more accurate, a child who is biologically related to at least one of them). Thus, they are no more in danger of commodifying the child than parents in general. But parents whose motivations are duplicative want specifically this child and no other, and this raises weighty questions. When we ask, why must it be this specific child, the answers are likely to hint at a view of the child as product, who will be valued primarily for his basketball prowess or her resemblance to a beloved relative.

With respect to this concern over commodification, it is interesting to ask why, in reproductive technology generally but especially in the debate over cloning, one so often sees the phrase "playing God," always assumed to have a negative slant. What does it mean to play God, and why is it necessarily a bad thing? There seems to be a very common human sense that there are certain limits on what we as humans ought to control. Some people express these limits in explicitly religious terms, while others might speak more generally of "fate" or "providence." One sees the same sort of fears when people express the idea that we humans ought not to "tamper" with evolution, as if evolution somehow "knows" where it is going and we are in danger of blundering in and messing up the plan.

Genetic enhancement, of individuals and of the human race as a whole, has captured the imagination of many ethicists at the beginning of the twenty-first century. If we can use genetic know-how to raise our children above the level to which they might naturally aspire, are we turning our children into commodities? Ethicists also worry about social justice—will the gap in our society between the haves and the have-nots, grow even greater if the "haves" can purchase certain inborn qualities for their kids? (We already see the results of certain parents being able to purchase straight teeth for their kids through orthodontia, and to make the most of their inborn intelligence through various kinds of academic coaching.) Others have the opposite concern: if some parents begin to enhance their kids, for example to provide them with above-average attention spans, will other parents feel that they must enhance *their* kids to keep up, and will the state eventually mandate the enhancement (in the same way that the state mandates required schooling and vaccination). Is state-mandated genetic enhancement ethically different from the abuses of twentieth-century eugenics? With our increased abilities to avoid children with disabilities and perhaps soon to choose children with extra abilities, we are moving, in the evocative phrase, "from chance to choice."[39]

Fears of genetic enhancement, or taking evolution into our own hands, are expressed in the popular culture in all sorts of ways, from the enduring attraction of the Frankenstein story to the Disney cartoon of the sorcerer's apprentice. The nickname of "Frankenfoods" given to genomically altered foodstuffs in Europe shows how near to the surface this kind of fear is.

What does it mean to play God with respect to children? It could mean to take total control and to create children instead of simply to love and accept the children we are given. The fears expressed about cloning and genetic enhancement are that parents will eventually be able to "order" custom-made children with a set of desired characteristics. (A cartoon I once saw sums up the unexpected dangers: Parents are approaching a genetics lab with unhappy expressions on their faces; they are pushing a stroller with a little boy who looks very much like Mickey Mouse. The lab technician is saying, "But you said you wanted a boy who resembled a famous movie star!") If parents could truly order ready-made children, they come perilously close to perceiving them almost entirely as means to the parents' ends. This could be morally disastrous.

On the other hand, there is within the Western religious tradition, and especially within Judaism, the notion of human beings as God's partners in creation. Elliot Dorff says:

> Cloning brings us back to the principles in the opening chapters of Genesis, defining our relationship to God and to God's universe. ... Adam and Eve are put into the Garden of Eden 'to work it and preserve it' (Genesis 2:15). ... In a parallel talmudic phrase, we are God's 'partners in the ongoing act of creation' when we improve the human lot in life.[40]

This tradition suggests it is immoral to fail to act, out of fear, when technological innovation would help to erase suffering. And if prospective parents see themselves not as the sole creators of their children, no matter how they are brought into being, but as cocreators with however they define that which is beyond them, it is entirely possible that they will continue to consider their children as separate, independent entities, with their own goals to attain.

In this context, it is worth taking a look at Frankenstein's monster, which has so haunted our technological nightmares, and comparing it to a more optimistic view of human scientific endeavor, as expressed in the sixteenth-century Jewish folk legend of the golem. Both stories depict men of extraordinary capabilities, who create human or quasi-human creatures who are in some sense quite clearly their "children." But whereas Dr. Frankenstein has become a modern synonym for the evil that results from an unbridled lust for power, the golem story suggests that creative power, rightly used, can be a moral obligation.

Frankenstein, as everybody knows, is a horror novel written in 1816 by Mary Shelley, as part of a contest among four friends to enliven a rainy holiday.[41] Dr. Frankenstein becomes enamored of the more arcane scientific arts and, while still a student, manages to create a human being in his attic lodgings. This new being, possessed of amazing intelligence but misshapen and untutored, eventually becomes so enraged at his pariah status that he murders the scientist's young brother, best friend, and, eventually, new bride. Shelley describes her protagonist as "a pale student of unhallowed arts" who "mock[s] the stupendous mechanism of the Creator of the world." [42]

For most of the novel, the single characteristic of young Frankenstein is his colossal lack of responsibility and moral sense. Frankenstein recognizes no limits to human endeavors, no sense of encroachment on sacred turf, he sees limits only as challenges to be broken for the sake of his own pride. He resembles a self-centered, irresponsible four-year-old. When he succeeds in creating the "monster" in his rooms, he is terrified by its weird aspect. He runs from his lodgings, spends the night on the street, and is tremendously relieved to return the next day and find the monster gone. He never expresses any concern about where it might be or what it might be up to, either in terms of its own needs for food and shelter or in terms of its danger to other people. He simply puts it out of his mind until years later, when he realizes that the "fiend" has killed Frankenstein's small brother.

Meanwhile, the poor monster, abandoned by his creator, has been having a terrible time. When he emerged, he had the form of an adult but the knowledge and skills of a newborn. Thrust into the world naked and alone, he nearly starves and freezes to death. Because of his hideous and terrifying aspect, he is stoned and persecuted wherever he goes. Nonetheless, he retains an essentially sweet and compassionate nature until he risks his life to rescue a drowning girl and is shot and wounded by a peasant for his efforts. All this the monster tells to his creator when he eventually confronts him, but Frankenstein is moved only for a moment. He concludes, "I was guiltless, but I had indeed drawn down a horrible curse upon my head, as mortal as that of crime." Only near the end of the novel does Frankenstein reluctantly accept responsibility for his creation, which he then proceeds to track (unsuccessfully) to the ends of the earth.

The Frankenstein legend has captured the Western imagination. At some point in our own century we largely forgot that the name Frankenstein belonged to the scientist, attaching it instead to the monster itself. To speak of "Frankenstein" is to express, in shorthand, our fears about technology "run amok."

Contrast the Frankenstein legend with that of the golem of Prague.[43] The golem is the creation of Rabbi Judah Loeb, a man as different from Dr. Frankenstein as it is possible to be. Rabbi Loeb, the religious leader of the Jewish ghetto in Prague in the sixteenth century, is a man of blazing moral rectitude. He is a renowned scholar and miracle worker, and there are many stories about how he saved his people, even before his birth.

At one point during Judah's reign as high rabbi, the Jewish people feel more threatened than usual. The elders of the community go to Rabbi Loeb for help. He prays long into the night and then falls asleep, during which time he dreams that he receives a command from heaven to create a golem to protect his people. Over the course of a week the rabbi and his disciples pray, fast, and go to the ritual bath. Finally, in the dead of night, they mold a creature from wet clay, and put in his mouth a paper on which they have written the name of God. The three men bow to all the cardinal points while pronouncing together the following: "Lord made a man from the clay of the earth and breathed the breath of life into his mouth." When they next look, they are no longer three but four: the golem has come to life.

In contrast to Frankenstein's immediate abandonment of his "offspring," Rabbi Judah names the golem Joseph, dresses him, and takes him home to live in his own home as a special servant, to be used only for the purpose of protecting the Jewish people. He does a very good job at this, especially since he has no need to sleep.

The golem story has an ambiguous ending. In all versions of the story he is killed by his creator. In one legend relationships between the Jews and Christians in Prague improve so much that Joseph's protection is no longer needed. In another the rabbi makes the mistake of saying one day, "I have no work for you, Joseph. Do whatever you please today." Joseph, like a small child, does what he pleases, which is to begin to wreck the houses in the ghetto. All the people call for Rabbi Loeb, who stops Joseph in his tracks by removing the name of God from his mouth. Supposedly the golem's clay remains still exist in the attic of the old Jewish synagogue in Prague, and various other stories recount the misadventures of lesser men than Rabbi Loeb who seek unsuccessfully to revivify the golem for their own selfish purposes.

I say the ending is ambiguous because, of course, the golem is destroyed (precisely what Dr. Frankenstein is unable to do in the novel). But the destruction has a positive aspect, because it assures listeners that the rabbi retains the power to control his creature and to put an end to it when it becomes a danger to mankind. The human (with God as partner) is in control even when the consequences are unforeseen and unintended. That same assurance might suggest that the creation of some genetically engineered foods does not have to send us hurtling down a slippery slope where everything we eat is ersatz, nor does cloning of humans for certain benign reasons, such as overcoming infertility, disempower us from refusing to clone for bad reasons, such as having a child who is exactly like one's favorite hero.

When Rabbi Loeb calls the golem into being (out of clay, as God created Adam) he is participating in an act of cocreation that is not only permitted by Judaism but required. Loeb improves his people's lot by providing them with a protector (as God told him to do in his dream). Thus, creating the golem is akin to "working and preserving" the Garden of Eden. The fact that Loeb and his students pray and fast before beginning their work, and that it is God's name itself written on parchment that animates the golem when it is inserted into his mouth, bespeaks Loeb's moral comfort with his act of creation. At every step in the story the rabbi is acting in partnership with God a complete contrast to Frankenstein, who is, in some perverse way, playing God.

The story of the golem can help us to see that creation does not necessarily lead to commodification. Parents who exert some control over the characteristics of their offspring are not necessarily doomed to limit their children's opportunities for an open future. Thus, I conclude that some, but not all, motivations for cloning are so likely to cause harm to the desired child that the practice can be entertained only with great caution. Because I see some uses of human cloning as ethically acceptable in the right situation, and because I agree with John Robertson[44] and Ronald Green[45] that those uses are likely to prevail, I do not conclude that cloning of humans should be banned. Instead, health professionals will have to act as gatekeepers, guided by policy statements of their professional societies, and refuse to offer cloning to couples who wish to employ it for reasons that appear likely to cause harm. It is even more important that should human reproductive cloning ever come to pass, prospective parents will need to educate themselves about the realities and pitfalls of this dramatically different reproductive technology.

Conclusion

ONE OF THE GREAT revolutions of the twentieth century was the ability of people to control the number and spacing of their offspring. This was a scientific revolution enabled by safer abortion techniques and new contraceptive modalities, but it was also a revolution in thinking, as large numbers of people, especially in the West, embraced the idea that the shape of their families was not a matter of fate or happenstance, or even god's will, but something that was subject to their decision.

Today, even while that earlier revolution has not yet penetrated to parts of the developing world, we are grappling with a different revolution: the ability to control not the quantity but the *qualities* of our children. My grandmother had to struggle for access to birth control. My mother, along with virtually all the women in her social group, took for granted that she would have two children, roughly four years apart. In contrast, my son and future daughter-in-law can also decide if they want boys or girls, or one of each, preceded as a matter of course by the genetic testing appropriate to our family history and ethnic group. Perhaps they will also decide to employ reproductive strategies to ensure that their children do not inherit my son's annoying allergies. And if, while they are at it, they have the opportunity to make sure that their children are not prone to obesity or acne or have unusual musical talent, should that be cause for concern? Isn't it just good parenting to want the best start for your kids that money can buy?

I began this book, in the Introduction, by talking about Celia, a woman with achondroplasia, and the increased choices genetic science offers people like her today as they decide how and whether to expand their families. But, as we saw throughout the book, genetic advances not only presents more options for people with disabilities, but they also present challenges to nondisabled people who might be interested in employing genetic techniques to mold their children to fit a specific image of their ideal family. In fact, these advances challenge and blur the very notion of what we mean by being "disabled" and what will count as the norm.

In previous generations, the focus was on having healthy children whose numbers and spacing did not overburden the ability of their parents to care for them. Even that seemingly innocuous norm has not failed to attract controversy. Disability activists, for example, have sometimes charged that using genetic testing and abortion to avoid the birth of children with disabilities devalues and disrespects the lives of people now living with those same conditions. Many pro-life activists share a worldview that is profoundly suspicious of what they see as an overemphasis on planning and control as well as on financial and educational preparations for parenthood.[1] Nonetheless, for the majority of Americans today, the use of family planning, infertility services, genetic counseling, and even abortion to avoid serious genetic defects is accepted as part of the reproductive landscape. In the twenty-first century, will we go on from there to actively control elements of our children that are not associated with gross norms of health and illness, but which instead attempt to fine-tune our families according to preconceived notions of exactly what kind of children we wish to have?

It is almost always true that new technologies raise new challenges for individuals and for societies as a while. The contraceptive technologies of the twentieth century were hailed by feminists because they gave women unprecedented control over their bodies and their lives. This biological control grounded an autonomy that enabled women to imagine futures for themselves as much more than wives and mothers—as astronauts and lawyers and construction workers also. Feminists hailed these technologies because they offered to both women and men the promise of a much more spacious future, with a much wider range of individual choice. As we struggle to grasp the moral meaning of the new genetic technologies of the twenty-first century, we should not lose sight of that goal. We should use these new technologies to ensure for our children, and for their children, not more constricted futures but more open ones.

Notes

Introduction

1. Adrienne Asch, "Reproductive Technology and Disability," in Sherrill Cohen and Nadine Taub, eds., *Reproductive Law for the 1990s* (Clifton, N.J.: Humana Press, 1989), 69–107.

2. Ibid.

3. Francis S. Collins, Eric D. Green, Alan E. Guttmacher, and Mark S. Guyer, "A Vision for the Future of Genomics Research," *Nature* 422 (2003): 835–47.

Chapter 1

1. Adrienne Asch, "Reproductive Technology and Disability," in Sherrill Cohen and Nadine Taub, eds., *Reproductive Laws for the 1990s* (Clifton, N.J.: Humana Press, 1989), 69–107.

2. Jay Katz, *The Silent World of Doctor and Patient* (New York, London: Free Press, Collier Macmillan, 1984).

3. Geoffrey Cowley, Elizabeth Leonard, Gregory Cerio, and Daniel Glick, "Made to Order Babies," *Newsweek*, winter 1990/spring 1991.

4. National Society of Genetic Counselors, "The Code of Ethics of the National Society of Genetic Counselors," *Journal of Genetic Counseling* 15, no. 5 (2006): 309–11.

5. David S. King, "Preimplantation Genetic Diagnosis and the 'New' Eugenics," *Journal of Medical Ethics* 25 (1999): 176–82.

6. Ibid., 177.

7. Ronald M. Green, *Babies by Design: The Ethics of Genetic Choice* (New Haven: Yale University Press, 2007), 130.

8. "Reconsidering 'Nondirectiveness' in Genetic Counseling," http://www.genesage.com/professionals/resources/answercenter/geneticcounseling.html. For a darker view of contemporary genetics and its eugenic tendencies, see King, "Preimplantation Genetic Diagnosis," 176–82.

9. Charles Bosk, "The Workplace Ideology of Genetic Counselors," in Dianne M. Bartels, Bonnie S. LeRoy and Arthur L. Caplan, eds., *Prescribing Our Future* (New York: Aldine de Gruyter, 1993), 25–38, 161.

10. "The Human Genome Project: New Tools for Tomorrow's Health Research." edited by National Institutes of Health: NIH 3190, 1992.

11. Nancy Wexler, "Clairvoyance and Caution: Repercussions from the Human Genome Project," in Daniel J. Kevles and Leroy Hood, eds., *The Code of Codes: Scientific and Social Issues in the Human Genome Project* (Cambridge, Mass.: Harvard University Press, 1992), 211–43, 211.

12. Dianne M. Bartels, "Preface," in Dianne M. Bartels, Bonnie S. LeRoy and Arthur L. Caplan, eds., *Prescribing Our Future: Ethical Challenges in Genetic Counseling* (New York: Aldine de Gruyter, 1992), ix–xiii.

13. Barbara Katz Rothman, *The Tentative Pregnancy: Prenatal Diagnosis and the Future of Motherhood* (New York: Viking, 1986), 40.

14. Luba Djurdjinovic, "Psychological Counseling," in Diane L. Baker, Jane L. Schuete and Wendy R. Uhlmann, eds., *A Guide to Genetic Counseling* (New York: Wiley-Liss, 1998), 127–66.

15. Rothman, *The Tentative Pregnancy*, 40.

16. Francis Collins, "Medical and Ethical Consequences of the Human Genome Project," *Journal of Clinical Ethics* 2 (Winter, 1990): 260–7, 261.

17. Tibor Scitovsky, "The Joyless Economy," in Gerald Dworkin, ed., *The Theory and Practice of Autonomy* (Cambridge: Cambridge University Press, 1988), 72–73.

18. Abby Lippman, "Prenatal Genetic Testing and Screening: Constructing Needs and Reinforcing Inequities," *American Journal of Law and Medicine* 17, no. 1–2 (1991): 15–50,19.

19. Robin J. R. Blatt, "To Choose or Refuse Prenatal Testing," *Gene WATCH,* January–February (1987): 3–5.

20. Lippman, "Prenatal Genetic Testing and Screening," 30–31.

21. Ibid., 23.

22. Larry Gostin, "Genetic Discrimination: The Use of Genetically Based Diagnostic and Prognostic Tests by Employers and Insurers," *American Journal of Law and Medicine* 17 (1991): 109–44.

23. King, "Preimplantation Genetic Diagnosis." 177–88.

24. Theresa M. Marteau and Harriet Drake, "Attributions for Disability: The Influence of Genetic Screening," *Social Science and Medicine* 40, no. 8 (1995): 1127–32, 1130.

25. Diane B. Paul, *The Politics of Heredity: Essays on Eugenics, Biomedicine, and the Nature-Nurture Debate* (Albany: State University of New York Press, 1988), 173–86. Paul points out that current medical advice is to keep children on the diet as long as possible, even through adolescence, but that financial help for parents is spotty. One survey in New York State found that only 10 percent of families eligible for Medicaid were eligible for assistance with the formula and foods required for the phenylketonuria (PKU) diet; a public program paid food costs for children in upstate New York but not in New York City, where only infants are covered.

26. Arthur L. Caplan, "The Ethics of Genetic Counseling," in Dianne M. Bartels, Bonnie S. Le Roy and Arthur L. Caplan, eds., *Prescribing Our Future* (New York: Aldine de Gruyter, 1993), 149–168, 161.

27. Walter Nance, "Parables," in Dianne M. Bartels, Bonnie S. LeRoy and Arthur L. Caplan, eds., *Prescribing Our Future* (New York: Aldine de Gruyter, 1993),89–96, 92.

28. Robert Wachbroit and David Wasserman, "Patient Autonomy and Value-Neutrality in Nondirective Genetic Counseling," *Stanford Law and Policy Review* 6 (1995): 103–22.

29. Mary Terrell White, "Making Responsible Decisions: An Interpretive Ethic for Genetic Decisionmaking," *Hastings Center Report* 29, no. 1 (1999): 14–21.

30. Albert R. Jonsen, "Foreword," in Edwin R. DuBose, Ronald P. Hamel and Laurence J. O'Connell, eds., *A Matter of Principles? Ferment in U.S. Bioethics*, (Valley Forge, Penn.: Trinity Press International, 1994), ix.

31. Joan H. Marks, "The Training of Genetic Counselors," in D. M. Bartels, B. LeRoy, and Arthur L. Caplan, eds., *Prescribing Our Future: Ethical Challenges in Genetic Counseling* (New York: Aldine de Gruyter, 1993) 15–24.

32. Joel Feinberg, "The Child's Right to an Open Future," in Will Aiden and Hugh La Follette, eds., *Whose Child? Children's Rights, Parental Authority, and State Power* (Totowa, N.J.: Littlefield, Adams, 1980), 124–53.

33. Ibid., 125–26.

34. John Locke, *Second Treatise of Government:* section 61.

35. *Prince v. Massachusetts*, 321 U.S. 170 (1944).

36. *Wisconsin v. Yoder*, 406 U.S. 205 (1972).

37. Ibid., 211–12.

38. Ibid., 222.

39. Ibid., 239–40 (J. White concurring).

40. Lainie Friedman Ross, *Children, Families, and Health Care Decision Making.* (Oxford, New York: Clarendon Press, Oxford University Press, 1995), 3.

41. William Galston, "Two Concepts of Liberalism," *Ethics* 105, no. 3 (1995): 516–34, 521.

42. Ibid., 523.

43. Martha C. Nussbaum, "Human Capabilities, Female Human Beings," in Martha C. Nussbaum and Jonathan Glover, eds., *Women, Culture, and Development: A Study of Human Capabilities* (Oxford, New York: Clarendon Press, Oxford University Press, 1995), 61–105, 81.

44. Ibid., 84.

45. Ibid., 85.

46. John Stuart Mill, *On Liberty: Annotated Text, Sources and Background, Criticism*, ed. David Spitz (New York: Norton, 1975), 55.

47. Ibid., 64.

48. Ibid.

49. Galston, "Two Concepts of Liberalism," 522.

50. Ronald M. Green, "Much Ado about Mutton: An Ethical Review of the Cloning Controversy," in Paul Lauritzen, ed., *Cloning and the Future of Human Embryo Research* (New York: Oxford University Press, 2000), 114–31.

51. Green, *Babies by Design*, 125.

52. Michael Sandel, "The Case against Perfection," *Atlantic Monthly* 292, no. 3 (2004): 50–4, 56–60, 62.

53. Eric Malmqvist, "Reproductive Technologies and the Question of the Child's Future Freedom," in S. Holm, J. Gunning, and I. Kenway, eds., *Ethics, Law and Society*, vol. IV (2009).

54. Rosamund Scott, *Choosing Between Possible Lives: Law and Ethics of Prenatal and Preimplantation Genetic Diagnosis* (Oxford, Portland, Ore.: Hart Publishing, 2007), 322.

55. Green, *Babies by Design,* 130.

56. Ibid., 129.

57. Bonnie Steinbock, "Sex Selection: Not Obviously Wrong," *Hastings Center Report* 32, no.1 (2001): 23–28.

58. http://microsort.net/

59. http://www.microsort.net/library/MSPatInfoPkt2.pdf

60. The Practice Committee of the American Society for Reproductive Medicine, "Use of Clomiphene Citrate in Women," *Fertility and Sterility* 80, no. 5 (2003): 1302– 1308.

61. Genetics and Public Policy Center. *Preimplantation Genetic Diagnosis: A Discussion of the Challenges, Concerns, and Preliminary Policy Options Related to the Genetic Testing of Human Embryos,* 2004, 3.

62. Denise Grady, "Birth Defects Tied to Fertility Techniques," *New York Times*, November 17, 2008.

63. Ibid., 5–6.

64. Ibid., 22.

65. Norbert Gleicher, Andrea Weghofer, and David Barad. "Preimplantation Genetic Screening: 'Established' and Ready for Prime Time?" *Fertility and Sterility* 89, no. 4 (2008): 780–88.

66. Sandel, "The Case against Perfection," 50–4, 56–60, 62.

67. For a nice discussion of instrumentalization, see Erik Malmqvist, "Analysing Our Qualms about 'Designing' Future Persons: Autonomy, Freedom of Choice, and Interfering with Nature," *Medicine, Health Care, and Philosophy* 10, no. 4 (2007): 407–416.

68. The President's Council on Bioethics. Beyond therapy—Biotechnology and the Pursuit of Happiness. Washington, D.C. October 2003. http://www.bioethics.gov

69. Immanuel Kant, ed., *Groundwork of the Metaphysics of Morals* (New York: Harper and Row, 1964), 96.

70. William Ruddick, "Parents and Life Prospects," in Onora O'Neill and William Ruddick, eds., *Having Children: Philosophical and Legal Reflections on Parenthood* (New York: Oxford University Press, 1979), 124–37.

Chapter 2

1. Bonnie Steinblock, "The Logical Case for 'Wrongful Life,'" *Hastings Center Report* 16 (1986): 15–20.

2. Dan W. Brock, "The Non-Identity Problem and Genetic Harms—The Case of Wrongful Handicaps," *Bioethics* 9 (1995): 269–75.

3. This is a variation of a famous hypothetical first put forth by Derek Parfit in *Reasons and Persons* (Oxford: Oxford University Press, 1984) and used in a slightly altered version by Dan Brock. Ibid., 270.

4. John A. Robertson, "Embryos, Families, and Procreative Liberty: The Legal Structure of the New Reproduction," *Southern California Law Review* 59 (1986): 987–1000.

5. Bonnie Steinblock and Ronald McClamrock, "When Is Birth Unfair to the Child," *Hastings Center Report* 24, no. 6 (1994): 15–22.

6. Robertson, "Embryos, Families, and Procreative Liberty," 987.

7. Walter Nance, "Parables," in D. M. Bartels, B. S. LeRoy and A. L. Caplan, eds., *Prescribing Our Future* (New York: Aldine de Gruyter, 1993), 92.

8. Arthur L. Caplan, "The Ethics of Genetic Counseling," in D. M. Bartels, B. S. LeRoy and A. L. Caplan, eds., *Prescribing Our Future* (New York: Aldine de Gruyter, 1993), 161.

9. John Harris, "Is there a coherent social conception of disability?" *Journal of Medical Ethics* 26 (2000): 95–100.

10. Matti Hayry, "There is a difference between selecting a deaf embryo and deafening a hearing child," *Journal of Medical Ethics* 30 (2004): 510–512.

11. Ibid., 510, emphasis in the original.

12. Gregory Crouch, "A Crusade Born of a Suffering Infant's Cry," *New York Times*, March 19, 2005.

13. Brock, "The Non-Identity Problem and Genetic Harms," 84.

14. Robertson, "Embryos, Families, and Procreative Liberty," 989.

15. Ibid., 991.

16. Ibid., 992–93

17. Liza Cohen, "Recovery of Limited Damages in Wrongful Pregnancy Action: *Johnson v. University Hospitals of Cleveland*," *Journal of Law and Health* 4 (1989–90): 83–109.

18. *Gleitman v. Cosgrove*, 49 N.J. 42 (1967).

19. *Procanik v. Cillo*, 97 N.J. 339 (1984).

20. Steinblock, "The Logical Case for 'Wrongful Life.'"

21. Ronald M. Green, "Much Ado about Mutton: An Ethical Review of the Cloning Controversy," in P. Lauritzen, ed., *Cloning and the Future of Human Embryo Research* (New York: Oxford University Press, 2000), 114–131.

22. Ronald M. Green, personal comment.

23. Brock, "The Non-Identity Problem and Genetic Harms," 274.

24. Ibid.

25. Ibid.

26. Joel Feinberg, *Harm to Others* (New York: Oxford University Press, 1984), 101.

27. Steinblock, "The Logical Case for 'Wrongful Life.'"

28. Cynthia B. Cohen, "'Give Me Children or I Shall Die!' New Reproductive Technologies and Harm to Children," *Hastings Center Report* 26, 2(1996): 19–27, 23.

29. Ibid., 23–24, emphasis in the original.

30. Ronald M. Green, "Parental Autonomy and the Obligation Not to Harm One's Child Genetically," *Journal of Law, Medicine and Ethics* 25 (1997): 5–15, 8.

31. The notion of a "slot" or "placeholder" is from R.I. Sikora and is quoted in David Heyd, *Genethics* (Berkeley: University of California Press, 1992).

32. Green, "Parental Autonomy," 8.

33. Ibid., 10.

34. Leon Kass, "The Wisdom of Repugnance," *The New Republic*, June 2, 1997, 17–27.

35. *Cloning Human Beings: Report and Recommendations of the National Bioethics Advisory Commission* (Rockville, Md.: The National Bioethics Advisory Commission, 1997), 1–62.

Chapter 3

1. Edward S. Cohn, Philip M. Kelley, and Thomas W. Fowler, "Clinical Studies of Families with Hearing Loss Attributable to the Mutations in the Connexin 26 Gene (GJB2/DFNB1)," *Pediatrics* 103, no. 3 (1997): 546–674.

2. Bonnie Poitras Tucker, "Deaf Culture, Cochlear Implants, and Elective Disability," *Hastings Center Report* 28, no. 4 (1998): 6–14, 6.

3. Jack R. Gannon, *The Week the World Heard Gallaudet* (Washington, D.C.: Gallaudet Press, 1989).

4. Lennard J. Davis, "Deafness and the Riddle of Identity," *Chronicle of Higher Education*, January 12, 2007, B6–B8.

5. "NIH Consensus Development Panel on Cochlear Implants in Adults and Children," *Journal of the American Medical Association* 274, no. 24 (1995): 1955–61; Amy Elizabeth Brusky, "Making Decisions for Deaf Children Regarding Cochlear Implants: The Legal Ramifications of Recognizing Deafness as a Culture Rather Than a Disability," *Wisconsin Law Review*, 1995, 235–70.

6. Edward Dolnick, "Deafness as Culture," *The Atlantic*, September 1993, 38.

7. Brusky, "Making Decisions for Deaf Children."

8. Harlan Lane and Michael Grodin, "Ethical Issues in Cochlear Implant Surgery: An Exploration into Disease, Disability, and the Best Interests of the Child," *Kennedy Institute of Ethics Journal* 7, no. 3 (1997): 231–52.

9. Brusky, "Making Decisions for Deaf Children."

10. Quoted in Lane and Grodin, "Ethical Issues in Cochlear Implant Surgery."

11. Ibid.

12. Ibid.

13. Brusky, "Making Decisions for Deaf Children."

14. Ibid.

15. Lane and Grodin, "Ethical Issues in Cochlear Implant Surgery."

16. Brusky, "Making Decisions for Deaf Children."

17. Carol Padden and Tom Humphries, *Deaf in America: Voices from a Culture* (Cambridge, Mass.: Harvard University Press, 1988).

18. John Christiansen, "Sociological Implications of Hearing Loss," paper presented at the *Genetics of Hearing Impairment*, Annals of the New York Academy of Sciences, New York, 1991.

19. Oliver Sacks, *Seeing Voices: A Journey into the World of the Deaf* (Berkeley: University of California Press, 1989).

20. Dolnick, "Deafness as Culture," 37–53, 38.

21. Lane and Grodin, "Ethical Issues in Cochlear Implant Surgery."

22. Liza Mundy, "A World of Their Own," *Washington Post*, March 31, 2002.

23. H-Dirksen L. Bauman, "Designing Deaf Babies and the Question of Disability," *The Journal of Deaf Studies and Deaf Education* 10 (2005): 311–15.

24. Ibid.

25. M. Spriggs, "Lesbian Couple Create a Child Who Is Deaf like Them," *Journal of Medical Ethics* 28 (2002): 283.

26. Tucker, "Deaf Culture, Cochlear Implants, and Elective Disability," 7.

27. Ibid.

28. Ibid., 9.

29. Stephen Lamar Winn, "Employment Outcomes for the Congenitally Deaf in Australia: Has Anything Changed?" *American Annals of the Deaf* 152, no. 4 (2007): 382–90.

30. Andrew Solomon, "Defiantly Deaf," *New York Times Magazine*, August 28, 1994, 43.

31. Leah Cohen, *Train Go Sorry: Inside a Deaf World* (New York: Vintage Books, 1995).

32. Nora Ellen Groce, *Everyone Here Spoke Sign Language: Hereditary Deafness on Martha's Vineyard* (Cambridge, Mass.: Harvard University Press, 1985).

33. Ibid., 3.

34. Ibid., 56.

35. Ibid., 62–66.

36. Ibid., 138.

37. Christiansen, "Sociological Implications of Hearing Loss."

38. Dolnick, "Deafness as Culture," 43.

39. Tom Shakespeare, *Disabilities Rights and Wrongs* (Oxford, UK: Routledge, 2006).

40. Quoted in Shakespeare, Ibid.

41. Shakespeare, *Disabilities Rights and Wrongs*, 55.

42. Ibid., 45.

43. Carina Dennis, "Deaf by Design," *Nature* 431, no. 21 (October 2004).

44. Dolnick, "Deafness as Culture," 40.

45. Solomon, "Defiantly Deaf," 65.

46. Dolnick, "Deafness as Culture," 520.

47. Judith Rich Harris, *The Nurture Assumption: Why Children Turn out the Way They Do* (New York: Free Press, 1998).

48. Gannon, *The Week the World Heard Gallaudet.*

49. Beryl Lieff Benderly, *Dancing without Music: Deafness in America* (Washington, D.C.: Gallaudet University Press, 1990).

50. Paul Preston, *Mother, Father Deaf: Living between Sound and Silence* (Cambridge, Mass.: Harvard University Press, 1994).

51. Harris, *The Nurture Assumption.*

52. Dennis, "Deaf by Design," 894.

53. Tucker, "Deaf Culture, Cochlear Implants, and Elective Disability," 7.

54. Kathleen Shaver Arnos, Jamie Israel, and Margaret Cunningham, "Genetic Counseling of the Deaf," *Annals of the New York Academy of Sciences,* 630, (1991): 212–22.

55. Anna Middleton, J. Hewison, and R. F. Mueller, "Attitudes of Deaf Adults toward Genetic Testing for Hereditary Deafness," *American Journal of Human genetics* 63, (1998): 1175–80.

56. K. Kalla, M. A. Pence, K. Osann, and A. P. Walker, "Hard of Hearing and Deaf Individuals' Knowledge and Interest in Genetic Counseling," in American Society Human Genetics annual meeting.

57. Dennis, "Deaf by Design," 896.

58. Susannah Baruch, David Kaufman, and Kathy L. Hudson. "Genetic Testing of Embryos: Practices and Perspectives of Us in Vitro Fertilization Clinics," *Fertility and Sterility* 89, no. 5 (2008): 1053–8.

59. Arnos, Israel, and Cunningham, "Genetic Counseling of the Deaf," 221.

60. Ibid., 213.

61. Ibid.

62. Ben Gose, "Pride Vs. Practicality: Critics of Gallaudet Say Its Emphasis on Deaf Identity Leaves Students Illiterate," *Chronicle of Higher Education*, March 29, 1996, 53–54.

63. William A. Galston, "Two Concepts of Liberalism," *Ethics* 105, no. 3 (1995): 516–34, 522.

64. Brusky, "Making Decisions for Deaf Children."

65. William Saletan, "Deformer Babies: The Deliberate Crippling of Children." *Slate,* September 21, 2006.

66. "Preimplantation Genetic Diagnosis: A Discussion of the Challenges, Concerns, and Preliminary Policy Options Related to the Genetic Testing of Human Embryos," (Baltimore, Md.: Genetics & Public Policy Center, 2004).

67. Bartha M. Knoppers and Rosario M. Isasi. "Regulatory Approaches to Reproductive Genetic Testing." *Human Reproduction* 19, no. 12 (2004): 2695–701.

68. S. Baruch, G. Javitt, J. Scott, and K. Hudson, *Reproductive Genetic Testing: Issues and Options for Policymakers* (Baltimore, Md.: Genetics & Public Policy Center, 2004).

69. "Public Attitudes to Fertility Treatment, Embryo Research and the Regulation of This Work—Preliminary Findings from the UK" (London: Human Fertilisation and Embryology Authority, 2004).

70. Alisa Taylor, "Debating Deafness and Embryo Selection: Are We Undermining Reproductive Confidence in the Deaf Community?" *BioNews.org.uk*, April 21 2008, http://www.bionews.org.uk. (accessed May 7, 2009)

71. Sarah-Kate Templeton, "Deaf Demand Right to Designer Deaf Children," *TIMESONLINE (from The Sunday Times)*, December 23, 2007.

72. Baruch, Javitt, Scott, and Hudson, *Reproductive Genetic Testing*, 3.

73. Ibid., 38.

74. Ibid., 42.

Chapter 4

1. Nancy Wexler, "Clairvoyance and Caution: Repercussions from the Human Genome Project," in Daniel J. Kevles and Leroy Hood, eds., *The Code of Codes: Scientific and Social Issues in the Human Genome Project* (Cambridge, Mass.: Harvard University Press, 1992), 211–43.

2. Catherine A. Hayes, "Genetic Testing for Huntington's Disease—A Family Issue," *New England Journal of Medicine* 327 (1992): 1449–53.

3. Albert Rosenfeld, "At Risk for Huntington's Disease: Who Should Know What and When?" *Hastings Center Report* 14, no. 3 (1984): 5–8.

4. Henry T. Greely, "Health Insurance, Employment Discrimination, and the Genetics Revolution," in Daniel J. Kevles and Leroy Hood, eds., *The Code of Codes: Scientific and Social Issues in the Human Genome Project* (Cambridge, Mass.: Harvard University Press, 1992).

5. "The Genetic Testing of Children," Report of a Working Party of the Clinical Genetics Society (UK), *Journal of Medical Ethics* 31 (1994): 331–44.

6. Ibid., 785–97; Sheila McLean, "Genetic Screening of Children: The U.K. Position," *Journal of Contemporary Health Law and Policy* 12 (1995): 117–30; ASHG/ACMG, "Points to Consider: Ethical, Legal, and Psychosocial Testing in Children and Adolescents," *American Journal of Human Genetics* 57, no. 5 (1995): 1233–41.

7. Pascal Borry, L. Stultiens, H. Nys, J-J. Cassiman, and K. Dierickx, "Presymptomatic and Predictive Genetic Testing in Minors: A Systematic Review of Guidelines and Position Papers," *Clinical Genetics* 70 (2006): 374–81.

8. Dorothy Wertz, H. Fanos, and P. R. Reilly, "Genetic Testing for Children and Adolescents: Who Decides?" *Journal of the American Medical Association* 272 (1994): 875–81.

9. Judith Granbois and Gail Vance, "Ethical Issues in Late Onset Genetic Disorders: Cases and Methods," presentation for the Association for Practical and Professional Ethics (APPE), March 1996.

10. Nancy Wexler, "The Tiresias Complex: Huntington's Disease as a Paradigm of Testing for Late-Onset Disorders," *Federation of American Societies for Experimental Biology Journal* 6 (1992): 2820–5, 2823.

11. ASHG/ACMG. "Points to Consider."

12. Ibid., 1238.

13. Eric D. Kodish, "Testing Children for Cancer Genes: The Rule of Earliest Onset," *Journal of Pediatrics* 135 (1999): 390–5.

14. Mary Z. Pelias, "Duty to Disclose in Medical Genetics: A Legal Perspective," *American Journal of Medical Genetics* 39 (1991): 347–53, 349.

15. Kimberly A. Quaid, Sharon L. Sims, Melinda M. Swenson, et al., "Living at Risk: Concealing Risk and Preserving Hope in Huntington Disease." *Journal of Genetic Counseling* 17, no. 1 (2007): 117–28.

16. Donna L. Dickenson, "Can Children and Young People Consent to Be Tested for Adult Onset Genetic Disorders?" *British Journal* 318 (1999): 1063–6.

17. Allyn McConkie-Rosell, Gail A. Spiridigliozzi, Elizabeth Melvin, Deborah V. Dawson, Ave M. Lachiewicz, "Living with Genetic Risk: Effect on Adolescent Self-Concept," *American Journal of Medical Genetics Part C* (Seminars in *Medical Genetics*) 148C (2008): 56–59.

18. Bernice S. Elger and Timothy W. Harding, "Testing Adolescents for a Hereditary Breast Cancer Gene (Brca1): Respecting Their Autonomy Is in Their Best Interest," *Archives of Pediatrics & Adolescent Medicine* 154, no. 2 (2006): 113–119.

19. American Academy of Pediatrics Committee on Genetics, "Molecular Genetic Testing in Pediatric Practice: A Subject Review," *Pediatrics* 106, no. 6 (2000): 1494–97.

20. President's Council on Bioethics, "The Changing Moral Focus of Newborn Screening: An Ethical Analysis by the President's Council on Bioethics," 2008.

21. "Code of Medical Ethics: Report of the Council on Ethical and Judicial Affairs." *American Medical Association*, 1995, 47.

22. L. McCabe, "Efficacy of a Targeted Genetic Screening Program for Adolescents (Invited Editorial)." *American Journal of Human Genetics* 31 (1994): 762–3.

23. Trisha Multhaupt-Buell, Anne Lovell, Lisa Mills, Kevin E. Stanford, Robert J. Hopkin, "Genetic Service Providers' Practices and Attitudes

Regarding Adolescent Genetic Testing for Carrier Status," *Genetics in Medicine* 9, no. 2 (2007): 101–04.

24. Sissela Bok, *Secrets* (New York: Vintage Books, 1989).

25. *Griswold v. Connecticut*, 381 U.S. 479 (1965).

26. Hilde Lindemann Nelson and James Lindemann Nelson, *The Patient in the Family: An Ethics of Medicine and Families* (New York: Routledge, 1995).

27. John Hardwig, "What about the Family?" *Hastings Center Report* 20, no. 2 (1990): 5–10.

28. Cynthia B. Cohen, "Moving Away from the Huntington's Paradigm in Predictive Genetic Testing of Children," in A. Clarke, ed., *The Genetic Testing of Children* (Oxford: Bios Publishers, 1998), 133–143, 136.

29. Fred Rosner, "Artificial Insemination in Jewish Law," in Fred Rosner and J. David Bleich, eds., *Jewish Bioethics* (New York: Hebrew Publishing Company, 1979), 105–17.

30. J. David Bleich, "Abortion in Halakhic Literature," in Fred Rosner and J. David Bleich, eds., *Jewish Bioethics* (New York: Sanhedrin Press, 1979), 134–77.

31. "Testimony of Rabbi Elliot N. Dorff, Laurie Zoloth, and Rabbi Moshe Tender." Paper presented at the 30th Meeting of the National Bioethics Advisory Commission, Georgetown University, May 7, 1999.

32. Rosner, "Artificial Insemination in Jewish Law,"105–17.

33. Bleich, "Abortion in Halakhic Literature," 134–77.

34. Fred Rosner, "Screening for Tay-Sachs Disease: A Note of Caution," *Journal of Clinical Ethics* 4 (1991): 251–52.

35. Dena S. Davis, "It Ain't Necessarily So: Clinicians, Bioethics, and Religious Studies," *Journal of Clinical Ethics* 5 (1994): 315–19.

36. Personal communication from Charles R. Scriver, Director of the Program, August 21, 1991.

37. J. Aronson, "Sound and Fury," (Artistic License Films in Association with Ronald Guttman and Nora Coblence Present a Production of Aronson Film Associates and Public Policy Productions in Association with Next Wave Films, 2001).

38. Lori Andrews, Jane Fullerton, Neil A. Holtzman and Arno G. Motulsky, eds., *Assessing Genetic Risks: Implications for Health and Social Policy* (Washington, D.C.: National Academy Press, 1994).

39. American Medical Association, Code of Medical Ethics.

40. Virginia A. Moyer, Ned Calonge, Steven M. Teutsch, Jeffrey R. Botkin, and on behalf of The United States Preventive Services Task Force, "Expanding Newborn Screening: Process, Policy, and Priorities," *Hastings Center Report* 38, no. 3 (2008): 32–39.

41. Ibid.

42. President's Council on Bioethics, "The Changing Moral Focus of Newborn Screening: An Ethical Analysis by the President's Council on Bioethics," 2008, 33.

43. Mary Ann Baily and Thomas H. Murray, "Ethics, Evidence, and Cost in Newborn Screening," *Hastings Center Report* 38, no. 3 (2008): 23–31.

44. President's Council on Bioethics, "The Changing Moral Focus of Newborn Screening," 52.

45. Ibid., 62.

46. Rebecca Koscik, P. K. Farrell and M. R. Kosorok, et al., "Cognitive Function of Children with Cystic Fibrosis: Deleterious Effects of Early Malnutrition," *Pediatrics* 113, no. 6 (2004): 1549–58; Philip M. Farrell, Michael R. Kosorok, Michael J. Rock, et al., "Early Diagnosis of Cystic Fibrosis through Neonatal Screening Prevents Severe Malnutrition and Improves Long-Term Growth," *Pediatrics* 107, no. 1 (2001): 1–13.

47. Donald B. Bailey, Jr., Debra Skinner, Arlene M. Davis, Ian Whitmarsh, and Cynthia Powell, "Ethical, Legal, and Social Concerns about Expanded Newborn Screening: Fragile X Syndrome as a Prototype for Emerging Issues," *Pediatrics* 121, no. 3 (2008): e693–e704.

48. Donald B. Bailey, Jr., Laura M. Beskow, Arlene M. Davis, and Debra Skinner, "Changing Perspectives on the Benefits of Newborn Screening," *Mental Retardation and Developmental Disabilities Research Reviews* 12 (2006): 270–79.

49. President's Council on Bioethics, "The Changing Moral Focus of Newborn Screening," 56.

50. Bailey, Beskow, Davis, and Skinner, "Changing Perspectives on the Benefits of Newborn Screening."

51. Elaine H. Mischler, Benjamin S. Wilfond, Norman Fost, et al., "Cystic Fibrosis Newborn Screening: Impact on Reproductive Behavior and Implications for Genetic Counseling," *Pediatrics* 102, no. 1 (1998): 44–52.

52. Roxanne Mykitiuk, "*Caveat Emptor:* Direct-to-Consumer Supply and Advertising of Genetic Testing," *Clinical and Investigative Medicine* 27, no. 1 (2004): 23–32.

53. A. J. Wolfberg, "Genes on the Web—Direct-to-Consumer Marketing of Genetic Testing," *New England Journal of Medicine* 355, no. 6 (2006): 543–5.

Chapter 5

1. April L. Cherry, "A Feminist Understanding of Sex-Selective Abortion: Solely a Matter of Choice?" *Wisconsin Women's law Journal* 10 (1995): 161–223.

2. Tabitha Powledge, "Unnatural Selection: On Choosing Children's Sex," in Helen B. Holmes, Betty B. Hoskins and Michael Gross, eds., *The Custom-Made Child? Women-Centered Perspectives* (Clifton, NJ: Humana Press, 1981), 193–200, 198.

3. A. Gentleman, "Indian Prime Minister denounces abortion of females," *New York Times*, April 29, 2008.

4. Haig H. Kazazian, Jr., "A Medical View," *Hastings Center Report* 10, no. 1 (1980): 17–18.

5. http://babygendermentor.com

6. Jill Colvin, "At-Home Test Shows Shows Sex of Fetus at 10 Weeks, Raises Worries of Gender-Linked Abortion," *Globe and Mail*, June 11, 2009.

7. Susannah Baruch, David Kaufman, Kathy L. Hudson, "Genetic testing of embryos: practices and perspectives of US in vitro fertilization clinics," *Fertility and Sterility* 89, no. 5 (2008): 1053–8.

8. Personal communication, Elizabeth Gettig, MS, CGC July 6, 2008.

9. Barbara Katz Rothman, *The Tentative Pregnancy: Prenatal Diagnosis and the Future of Motherhood* (New York: Viking, 1986).

10. Alison Dundes Renteln, "Sex Selection and Reproductive Freedom," *Women's Studies International Forum* 15, no. 3 (1992): 405–26.

11. J. Berkowitz, "Two Boys and a Girl Please and Hold the Mustard," *Public Health* 114 (2000): 5–7.

12. Michael Bayles, *Reproductive Ethics* (Englewood Cliffs, NJ: Prentice Hall, 1984); Gena Corea, *The Mother Machine: Reproductive Technologies*

from Artificial Insemination to Artificial Wombs. New York: Harper and Row, 1985), 199–201.

13. http://microsort.net/

14. Gina Kolata, "Researchers Report Success in Method to Pick Baby's Sex," *New York Times*, September 9, 1998.

15. http://microsort.net//

16. The President's Council on Bioethics. *Beyond therapy—Biotechnology and the Pursuit of Happiness.* A report of The President's Council on Bioethics, Washington, D.C. 2003.

17. Rothman, *The Tentative Pregnancy*, 133; Corea, *The Mother Machine*, 190–192.

18. Rothman, *The Tentative Pregnancy*, 136.

19. Margaret Atwood, *The Handmaid's Tale* (Boston: Hough Mifflin, 1986).

20. Marcia Guttentag and Paul F. Secord, *Too Many Women? The Sex Ratio Question* (Beverly Hills: Sage Publications, 1983).

21. Ted Plafker, "Sex Selection in China Sees 117 Boys Born for Every 100 Girls," *British Medical Journal* 324 (May 25, 2002): 1233.

22. Ibid.

23. Joseph Chamie, "The Global Abortion Bind," *YaleGlobal,* May 29, 2008.

24. Robyn Rowland, "Motherhood, Patriarchal Power, Alienation, and the Issue Of 'Choice' in Sex Preselection," in Gena Corea, ed., *Man-Made Women: How Reproductive Technologies Affect Women* (Bloomington: Indiana University Press, 1987), 74–87, 83.

25. Radhika Balakrishnan, "The Social Context of Sex Selection and the Politics of Abortion in India," in Gita Sen and Rachel C. Snow, eds., *Power and Decision: The Social Control of Reproduction* (Cambridge, Mass.: Harvard School of Public health, 1994), 267–86, 268.

26. Ibid., 26.

27. Gentleman, "Indian Prime Minister denounces abortion of females."

28. Elisabeth Bumiller, "No More Little Girls: Female Infanticide among the Poor of Tamil Nadu and Sex-Selective Abortion among the Rich of Bombay," *May You Be the Mother of a Hundred Sons: A Journey among the Women of India* (New York: Random House, 1990) 101–24.

29. Ibid., 101–24.

30. Michael S. Pollard and Philip S. Morgan, "Emerging Parental Gender Indifference? Sex Composition of Children and the Third Birth," *American Sociological Review* 67 (August, 2002): 600–13, 601.

31. Bumiller, "No More Little Girls," 101–24.

32. Madhu Kishwar, "The Continuing Deficit of Women in India and the Impact of Amniocentesis," in Gena Corea, ed., *Man-Made Women: How Reproductive Technologies Affect Women*, Bloomington: Indiana University Press, 1987) 30–7.

33. Nicholas D. Kristof, "Stark Data on Women: 100 Million Are Missing," *New York Times*, November 5, 1991.

34. Balakrishnan, "The Social Context of Sex Selection and the Politics of Abortion in India," 68.

35. Fred Arnold, Sunita Kishor, T. K. Roy, "Sex-Selective Abortions in India," *Population and Development Review* 28, no. 4 (2002): 759–85, 759.

36. Tai-Hun Kim, "The Effects of Sex-Selective Abortion on Fertility Level in Korea," *Korea Journal of Population and Development* 26, no. 1 (1997): 43–60, 45.

37. Monica Das Gupta and P. N. Mari Bhat, "Fertility Decline and Increased Manifestation of Sex Bias in India," *Population Studies* 51 (1997): 307–15, 307.

38. Corea, *The Mother Machine*, 210.

39. Helen Bequaert Holmes, "Choosing Children's Sex: Challenges to Feminist Ethics," in Joan Callahan, ed., *Reproduction, Ethics, and the Law* (Bloomington: Indiana University Press, 1995), 148–177, 153.

40. Gerald Meier, *Leading Issues in Economic Development*, 3rd ed. (New York: Oxford University Press, 1984) 576–8.

41. Hank Hyena, "Japanese Want Baby Girls; Indians Choose Boys." www.salon.com/health/sex/urge/world/1999/11/18/gender/index.html (accessed April 7, 2009).

42. Choe Sang-Hun, "Where Boys Were Kings, a Shift toward Baby Girls," *New York Times*, December 23, 2007.

43. Norimitsu Onishi, "Wed to Strangers, Vietnamese Wives Try to Build Korean Lives," *New York Times*, March 30, 2008, 6.

44. Sam Roberts, "U.S. births hint at bias for boys in some Asians," June 15, 2009.

45. Bayles, *Reproductive Ethics*, 34–36.

46. Amitai Etzioni, "Sex Control, Science, and Society." *Science* 161 (1968):1107–12, 1109.

47. Roberta Steinbacher and Faith Gilroy, "Sex Selection Technology: A Prediction of Its Use and Effect," *The Journal of Psychology* 124, no. 3 (1990): 283–88.

48. Nancy Plevin, "Parents Take a Thorny Ethical Path in Quest to Select Sex of Children," *Los Angeles Times*, June 14, 1992.

49. Lisa Belkin, "Getting the Girl," *New York Times Magazine*, July 25, 1999, 30.

50. Ibid.

51. Pollard and Morgan, "Emerging Parental Gender Indifference?" 600–613.

52. N. Gleicher and D. H. Barad, "The Choice of Gender: Is Elective Gender Selection, Indeed, Sexist?" *Human Reproduction* 22, no. 11 (2007): 3038–41.

53. Edgar Dahl, Ruchi S Gupta, Manfred Beutel, et al., "Preconception Sex Selection Demand and Preferences in the United States," *Fertility and Sterility* 85, no. 2 (2006): 468–473.

54. Bayles, *Reproductive Ethics*, 34–36.

55. Dorothy Wertz and John Fletcher, "Fatal Knowledge? Prenatal Diagnosis and Sex Selection," *Hastings Center Report* 19, no. 3 (1989): 21–27, 25.

56. Maura Ryan, "The Argument for Unlimited Procreative Liberty: A Feminist Critique," in Courtney Campbell, ed., *What Price Parenthood? Ethics and Assisted Reproduction* (Aldershot and Brookfield: Dartmouth, 1992), 84–90, 86.

57. Michael J. Sandel, "The case against perfection," *Atlantic Monthly* 292, no. 3(2004): 50–4, 56–60, 62.

58. J. Savulescu, "In defense of selection or nondisease genes," *American Journal of Bioethics* 1, no. 1 (2001): 16–19.

59. Wertz and Fletcher, "Fatal Knowledge? Prenatal Diagnosis and Sex Selectio," 26–7.

60. Barbara Katz Rothman, *Genetic Maps and Human Imaginations: The Limits of Science in Understanding Who We Are* (New York: Norton, 1998).

61. Belkin, "Getting the Girl," 30.

62. Rothman, *The Tentative Pregnancy*, 138.

63. Victoria Seavilleklein and Susan Sherwin, "The Myth of the Gendered Chromosome: Sex Selection and the Social Interest." *Cambridge Quarterly of Healthcare Ethics* 16 (2007): 7–19, 11.

64. Letty Cottin Pogrebin, *Growing up Free: Raising Your Child in the 80s*, (New York: McGraw-Hill, 1980).

65. Ryan, "The Argument for Unlimited Procreative Liberty."

66. Rothman, *The Tentative Pregnancy*, 121–23.

67. Ibid., 124–27.

68. Holmes, "Choosing Children's Sex," 136.

69. Pogrebin, *Growing up Free*, 123–127.

70. Rothman, *The Tentative Pregnancy*. 130.

71. Ibid., 122.

72. Wertz and Fletcher, "Fatal Knowledge? Prenatal Diagnosis and Sex Selection." 26–7.

73. Rothman, *The Tentative Pregnancy*. 122.

Chapter 6

1. John A. Robertson, "The Question of Human Cloning," *Hastings Center Report* 24, no. 2 (1994): 6.

2. National Human Genome Research Institute, "Cloning," http://www.genome.gov/25020028#7.(accessed May 7, 2009).

3. Gail H. Javitt, Kristen Suthers, and Kathy L. Hudson, *Cloning: A Policy Analysis* (Washington, D.C.: Genetics & Public Policy Center, 2006).

4. National Bioethics Advisory Commission, *Cloning Human Beings: Report and Recommendations of the National Bioethics Advisory Commission*, 1:62. (Rockville, Md.: National Bioethics Advisory Commission, 1997).

5. It appears that the number of times embryos can be split is curtailed by natural limits on their totipotency, which degrades after two or three cell divisions. Jacques Cohen and Giles Tomkin, "The Science, Fiction, and Reality of Embryo Cloning," *Kennedy Institute of Ethics Journal* 4, no. 3 (1994): 193–203.

6. Ibid., 196.

7. Ruth Macklin, "Splitting Embryos on the Slippery Slope," *Kennedy Institute of Ethics Journal* 4, no. 3 (1994): 209–25, 210.

8. A. Salkever, "Another Cloning First: This Time, a Monkey," *Christian Science Monitor*, January 14, 2000.

9. Thomas H. Murray, *The Worth of a Child* (Berkeley: University of California Press, 1996).

10. Insoo Hyun and Kyu Won Jung, "Human Research Cloning, Embryos, and Embryo-Like Artifacts," *Hastings Center Report* 36, no. 5 (2006), 34–41.

11. Abby Goudnough, "In the Park, a Usually Tough Crowd Bares Hearts for Diana," *New York Times*, September 15, 1997.

12. Leon R. Kass, "The Wisdom of Repugnance," *The New Republic*, June 2, 1997, 17–27.

13. Jean Bethke Elshtain, "Ewgenics," *The New Republic*, March 31, 1997, 25.

14. I owe this insight to Paul Root Wolpe, who also made me aware of Elshtain's article.

15. Arthur Caplan quoted in Macklin, "Splitting Embryos," 210.

16. Elshtain, "Ewgenics," 25.

17. Sheryl Gay Stolberg, "Buying Years for Women on the Biological Clock," *New York Times*, October 3, 1999.

18. Samantha Besson, "Enforcing the Child's Right to Know Her Origins: Contrasting Approaches under the Convention on the Rights of the Child and the European Convention on Human Rights," *Law, Policy and the Family* 21, no. 2 (2007) 137–159, 138.

19. Karen Lebacqz, "Genes, Justice, and Clones," in Ronald Cole-Turner, ed., *Human Cloning: Religious Responses* (Louisville: Westminster/John Knox, 1997), 49–57.

20. David Orentlicher, "Cloning and the Preservation of Family Integrity," *Louisiana Law Review* 59 (1998), 1019–40.

21. Murray, *The Worth of a Child*.

22. Vincent Kiernan, "The Morality of Cloning Humans: Theologians and Philosophers Offer Provocative Arguments," *The Chronicle of Higher Education*, July 18, 1997, 13–14.

23. John A. Robertson, "Liberty, Identity, and Human Cloning," *Texas Law Review* 76, no. 6 (1998): 1371–1456, 1373.

24. Kass, "The Wisdom of Repugnance," 17–27.

25. Hans Jonas, "Biological Engineering—a Preview," in *Philosophical Essays: From Ancient Creed to Technological Man* (Englewood Cliffs, N.J.: Prentice-Hall, 1974),141–167, 159.

26. Ibid., 161.

27. Ibid., 161–62.

28. Ibid.

29. Ibid., 162.

30. Robertson, "Liberty, Identity, and Human Cloning," 1417, n. 161.

31. Tom Jones, "Plant a Radish," in The Fantasticks (MGM Records, 1960).

32. Kass, "The Wisdom of Repugnance," 17–27.

33. Dan W. Brock, "Cloning Human Beings: An Assessment of the Ethical Issues Pro and Con," in Martha C. Nussbaum and Cass R. Sunstein, ed., *Clones and Clones; Facts and Fantasies about Human Cloning* (New York: Norton, 1998), 141–164, 154.

34. Soren Holm, "A Life in the Shadow: One Reason Why We Should Not Clone Humans," *Cambridge Quarterly of Healthcare Ethics* 7 (1998): 160–62.

35. Ibid.

36. Ibid.

37. National Bioethics Advisory Commission, *Cloning Human Beings: Report and Recommendations of the National Bioethics Advisory Commission* (Rockville, Md.: The National Bioethics Advisory Commission, 1997), 73.

38. Allan Verhey, "Commodification, Commercialization, and Embodiment," *Women's Health Issues* 7 (May–June 1997), 132.

39. Allen Buchanan, Norman Daniels, Daniel Wikler, Dan W. Brock, and Daniel I. Wilker, *From Chance to Choice: Genetics and Justice* (Cambridge: Cambridge University Press, 2000).

40. Elliott Dorff, *Matters of Life and Death: A Jewish Approach to Modern Medical Ethics* (Philadelphia: Jewish Publication Society, 1998).

41. Mary Shelley, *Frankenstein: Or, the Modern Prometheus* (New York: Signet, 1983).

42. Ibid., x–xi.

43. Accounts of the golem can be found in a number of books. See Dena S. Davis, "Religious Attitudes toward Cloning: A Tale of Two Creatures," *Hofstra Law Review* 27, no. 3 (1999): 509–21.

44. John A. Robertson, "Human Cloning and the Challenge of Regulation." *New England Journal of Medicine* 339 (July 1998): 119–22.

45. Ronald M. Green, "Much Ado about Mutton: An Ethical Review of the Cloning Controversy," in Paul Lauritzen, ed., *Cloning and the Future of Human Embryo Research* (New York: Oxford University Press, 2000), 114–131.

Conclusion

1. Kristin Luker, *Abortion and the Politics of Motherhood* (Berkeley: University of California Press, 1984).

INDEX